AF772218

Frank Ecker

Information Risk and Long-Run Performance of Initial Public Offerings

GABLER EDITION WISSENSCHAFT

Frank Ecker

Information Risk and Long-Run Performance of Initial Public Offerings

With forewords by Prof. Dr. Hellmuth Milde
and Prof. Dr. Per Olsson

GABLER EDITION WISSENSCHAFT

Bibliographic information published by the Deutsche Nationalbibliothek
The Deutsche Nationalbibliothek lists this publication in the Deutsche Nationalbibliografie; detailed bibliographic data are available in the Internet at http://dnb.d-nb.de.

Dissertation am Fachbereich IV der Universität Trier, 2005

1st Edition 2008

Editorial Office: Frauke Schindler / Anita Wilke

Gabler is part of the specialist publishing group Springer Science+Business Media.
www.gabler.de

Cover design: Regine Zimmer, Dipl.-Designerin, Frankfurt/Main
Printed on acid-free paper
Printed in Germany

ISBN 978-3-8349-1259-6

Foreword

Exactly forty years after Eugene Fama's (1965) article "The Behavior of Stock Market Prices" (Journal of Business), the play "Efficient Capital Markets" is still going strong. With his thesis, Frank Ecker is adding a new act to the play: His work is a combination of several new developments on the analytical and empirical capital market research front.

Capital market efficiency is based on two aspects. First, the ability of investors to identify a situation in which asset prices are out of the capital market equilibrium. Second, on the possibility of the market to make arbitrage profits by driving the prices back to the equilibrium value. Both aspects are conditional on the set of "relevant" information. As a result, the basic question is: What is relevant information and how is it processed by investors?

This work is building on the concept of information quality, information uncertainty or information risk. Fama's efficient market hypothesis is just a special case based on the assumption that new information is absolutely correct and completely credible to all investors. In contrast, this work makes use of the more general assumption that new information can be characterized by very different degrees of credibility, or quality. The setting of initial public offerings is chosen as one of the few capital market transactions arguably characterized by high information asymmetry between the firm's insiders (management) and outsiders (investors). As these investors know that they are at an informational disadvantage, they will only impute an *expected* and potentially incorrect information risk premium into the stock price. After the IPO, as new information is revealed over time, a signalling process by the firm starts, gradually allowing investors to update their belief on the firm's true information risk and therefore the firm's expected rate of return in a Bayesian sense.

While many explanations for the possible long-run underperformance of IPOs have been proposed in the literature, Frank Ecker hypothesizes that cross-sectional differences in the information risk surprise (positive and negative) drive the cross-sectional differences in stock market performance, an explanation that is actually consistent with efficient capital markets under information uncertainty. This work provides new evidence on the magnitude and the persistence of this updating process.

Hellmuth Milde

Foreword

In his work, Frank Ecker connects two strands of literature in the information economics / financial economics / accounting research areas: the stock market pricing of information uncertainty and the long-run performance of initial public offerings (IPOs).

The pricing of information risk and information uncertainty is at the forefront of today's asset pricing research. The traditional view of market efficiency holds that stock prices always incorporate all available information. Consequently, the quality of information cannot matter: Whether information quality is good or bad, everybody has access to the market price, which serves as an aggregator of all value relevant information. However, in a world where new information about a firm arrives and is expected to continue arriving in the future, the question as to how, and how fast, that information gets into price becomes pertinent. Specifically, if the public information is not of perfect quality, we can no longer be assured that someone else will not have access to better information at the next information release, i.e. as investors, we can be rationally afraid of ending up on the wrong side of information asymmetries. Certainly a risk one would want compensation for. In her 2003 Presidential Address to the American Finance Association, Maureen O'Hara laid out the arguments in an intuitive way: "Traders with superior information will move prices toward full information levels, but continuously attaining full information levels is not credible - new information arrives, old information becomes stale, and even informed traders may face risks that their information is obsolete. Market prices can be martingales with respect to information, but if traders have diverse information sets, then these expectations need not be the same across traders. Thus, as in microstructure models, the adjustment of prices to full information values can differ widely across markets that are deemed efficient." Easley and O'Hara (2004) continue to show how such information effects may not be diversified away in equilibrium. They argue that information risk effects are systematic in the pricing of stocks, i.e. part of required return, in spite of the fact that firm-specific information by definition is idiosyncratic.

The arguments referenced above are not uncontroversial. Other researchers argue that it is the overall precision of information rather than information asymmetries that affects required returns. The empirical facts, on the other hand, are fairly well established. Study after study show that different measures of information risk and/or information quality have economically and statistically significant predictive power over stock prices and stock returns (e.g., Easley et al. 2002, Francis et al. 2004, 2005). Firms with high information uncertainty have higher required returns and lower prices, also after controlling for all other factors that we know affect returns and prices (such as beta, size, book-to-market ratios, etc.).

Frank Ecker builds on the evidence regarding information uncertainty and identifies a situation where information uncertainty effects are likely to be at their most severe: when firms first start public trading, i.e., at their initial public offerings (IPOs). Frank Ecker starts with the presumption that investors are rational in a Bayesian sense. If they underestimate information uncertainty before the IPO, their initial required return is too low, and price is too high. As investors gradually get more and more information signals and can evaluate the firm-specific information risk, they will adjust the required return upwards, causing a drawn-out price adjustment: negative abnormal returns. The opposite will hold true if investors initially overestimate an IPO firm's information uncertainty. Thus, Frank Ecker's main argument can be described as a price adjustment process towards full information pricing in a situation where information is initially very sparse. The idea is quite novel – it essentially takes the results from the literature about required returns and applies it to a situation where there are abnormal returns, thus showing that there is a rational explanation for what has hitherto been described as irrational in the literature: the long-term abnormal returns following firms' IPOs.

Frank Ecker's work is the first text to put forth and test a theory for the long-term performance of IPO firms that builds on rational expectations, yet can accommodate long-term abnormal returns. Importantly, it is also the first test that fully explores cross-sectional variation in abnormal returns following firms' IPOs. Thus, we are left with a cohesive story that builds on rational investor behavior, supported by robust empirical evidence.

Per Olsson

Preface

I would like to express my gratitude to many people who contributed to this work: Professor Hartmut Wächter presided over my defense. My colleagues at the Swedish Institute for Financial Research in Stockholm commented on an early outline of the research idea. Professors Jennifer Francis and Katherine Schipper provided very helpful advice on the research design and writing issues. I profited from the continuous advice and encouragement from Professor Per Olsson, both during and after my visit at Duke University. Finally, I thank my advisor Professor Hellmuth Milde for the helpful discussions and his support and encouragement to visit the Duke PhD program. Professors Milde and Olsson also wrote the dissertation reports.

Frank Ecker

Contents

Foreword v

Foreword vii

Preface ix

List of Tables xiii

List of Figures xv

Symbols and Abbreviations xvii

1 Introduction and Motivation 1

2 Valuation under Information Risk 7

2.1 Classification of information risk 7

2.2 Empirical measurement of information risk 8

2.3 Conceptual consequences of the introduction of information risk 12

3 Derivation of a Returns-Based Measure of Information Quality 15

4 Abnormal Returns Measurement and Hypotheses Development 25

4.1 Methodological issues in long-term abnormal returns measurement . . . 25

4.1.1 What return is normal? 25

4.1.2 Choosing the right metric 33

4.1.3 Event-time vs. calendar-time approaches 37

4.1.4 Concluding remarks and problems discussion 40

4.2 Explaining abnormal IPO performance 43

5 Tests with Abnormal Portfolio Returns 51

5.1 Construction of the IPO sample 51

5.2 Calendar-time portfolios from the full IPO sample 55

5.3 Persistence tests 61

5.4 Deviation tests 68

5.4.1 Main results 68

5.4.2 The role of size 76

5.4.3 Analysis of subperiods 83

6 Robustness Tests **85**

6.1 Varying the calendar-time approach 85

6.2 Firm-specific tests 86

6.2.1 Deviation and IPO firm characteristics 89

6.2.2 Firm-specific abnormal return and size 91

6.2.3 Firm-specific abnormal return and operating performance 92

6.3 Further Robustness Tests 93

7 Concluding Remarks **97**

Appendix **99**

Bibliography **127**

List of Tables

1 Descriptive statistics for selected financial variables 20

2 Comparison of e-Loadings of Event Firms with Non-Event Firms 24

3 Distribution of IPO Sample by Year and Industry 53

4 Descriptive Statistics on Calendar-Time Portfolios 57

5 Abnormal Returns on IPO Portfolios (3-Factor Model) 60

6 Abnormal Returns on IPO Portfolios (4-Factor Model) 62

7 Abnormal Returns on Equal-weighted Portfolios For Separate Firm Ages 64

8 Descriptive Statistics on E-Loadings, Industry Averages and Deviation 68

9 Description of The Deviation-Quartile Calendar-Time Portfolios 70

10 Abnormal Return for Value-Weighted Deviation Quartile Portfolios . . 72

11 Abnormal Return for Equal-Weighted Deviation Quartile Portfolios . . 74

12 Factor Loadings from Regressions on Equal-weighted Portfolio Returns 75

13 Abnormal Value-Weighted Portfolio Returns per Deviation and Size Quartiles (OLS) 79

14 Abnormal Value-Weighted Portfolio Returns per Calendar-Time Quartile 84

15 Abnormal Portfolio Returns per Deviation Quartile – Jaffe-Mandelker Method (3-Factor) 87

16 Abnormal Portfolio Returns per Deviation Quartile – Jaffe-Mandelker Method (4-Factor) 88

17 Firm Age Regressions 90

18 Size Regressions 92

19 Operating Performance Regressions 94

20 Significance of the Difference Between Highest- and Lowest-Deviation Quartiles 96

A.1 Abnormal Portfolio Returns for Rolling Short Investment Horizons (3-factor) 101

A.2 Abnormal Portfolio Returns for Rolling Short Investment Horizons (4-factor) 107

A.3 Abnormal Return for Value-Weighted Deviation Quartile Portfolios (GARCH) 113

A.4 Abnormal Return for Equal-Weighted Deviation Quartile Portfolios (GARCH) 114

A.5 Abnormal Value-Weighted Portfolio Returns per Deviation and Size Quartiles (GARCH) 115

A.6 Abnormal Equal-Weighted Portfolio Returns per Deviation and Size Quartiles (OLS) 119

A.7 Abnormal Equal-Weighted Portfolio Returns per Deviation and Size Quartiles (GARCH) 123

List of Figures

1 Abnormal Portfolio Returns for Rolling Short Investment Horizons (OLS) (3-factor) 66

2 Abnormal Portfolio Returns for Rolling Short Investment Horizons (OLS) (4-factor) 67

A.1 Abnormal Portfolio Returns for Rolling Short Investment Horizons (GARCH) 99

A.2 Abnormal Portfolio Returns for Rolling Short Investment Horizons (4-factor) (GARCH) 100

Symbols and Abbreviations

#	Number (of)
%ile	Percentile
AAR	Average abnormal return
AMEX	American Stock Exchange
AQ	Accruals quality
BHAR	Buy-and-hold abnormal return
BM	Book-to-market (value of equity)
CAPM	Capital asset pricing model
CAR	Cumulative abnormal return
Coeff.	Coefficient
CRSP	Center for Research in Security Prices
DCA	Discretionary current accruals
EW	Equal-weighted
Exc.	Excess (return)
GARCH	Generalized autoregressive conditional heteroscedasticity
HML	High-Minus-Low factor
IPO	Initial public offering
NASDAQ	National Association of Securities Dealers Automated Quotation (system)
NPV	Net present value
NYSE	New York Stock Exchange
Obs.	Observations
OLS	Ordinary least squares
SDC	Securities Data Company
SEO	Seasoned equity offering
SIC	Security Industry Classification (code)
SMB	Small-Minus-Big factor
Std. dev.	Standard deviation
VW	Value-weighted

1. Introduction and Motivation

There is a long-standing debate in the financial economics literature about long-term abnormal stock returns following firms' initial public offerings (IPOs). Starting with Ritter (1991), this debate has concentrated on long-term underperformance, i.e., negative abnormal returns. He showed that the average IPO firm has a negative abnormal return over three years after the initial listing. Several researchers (see, e.g., Fama 1998) have voiced methodological and conceptual concerns about this finding, spurring the development of alternative techniques to correct for specific shortcomings. Largely, the more recent articles have not been able to document significantly negative abnormal returns on average.

Regardless of whether or not the average IPO firm underperforms, individual firms do exhibit negative as well as positive long-term abnormal returns. I add to the literature by offering and testing an explanation for why abnormal performance of IPO stocks, positive for some firms, negative for others, exists. To be more specific, this work explores whether cross-sectional differences in the abnormal performance of initial public offerings can be explained by deviations between ex-ante expected and ex-post realized information risk. In short, consistent with the rational expectations hypothesis, investors correctly assess the information risk of the average IPO. Consequently, I find no abnormal performance for the average firm in my sample. In situations where information risk has initially been underestimated, however, abnormal returns are significantly negative during the price adjustment process. When information risk has been overestimated, abnormal returns are significantly positive.

Information risk has recently been in the focus of both theoretical and empirical asset pricing research. O'Hara (2003), Easley and O'Hara (2004), and Lambert, Leuz, and Verrecchia (2006) model the role of information risk in the determination of expected returns. They show that firm-specific information risk cannot be diversified away and, for this reason, should be priced by investors. The pricing of information risk is empirically supported by Francis, LaFond, Olsson, and Schipper (2004a, 2005). Using different earnings quality metrics as proxies, they provide evidence of higher (lower) information risk being associated with higher (lower) expected returns for both equity and debt financing.

I argue that, in contrast to seasoned firms, the information risk of IPO firms cannot be properly assessed by investors at the time of the offering because of the lack of firm-specific information in the period preceding the offering. To be able to draw general inferences on the credibility (or quality) of information, it is essential to learn how the firm's disclosures map into subsequent realizations. Intuitively, this is not feasible in an IPO setting. Firms have to provide one to three financial statements in the offering prospectus (Teoh, Welch, and Wong 1998). However, their usefulness for the assessment of information risk is limited for at least two reasons. First, firms are allowed to alter originally applied accounting choices when preparing the statements for the offering prospectus. Second, and more importantly, there are generally few or no public announcements and/or records of public announcements for the period preceding the public offering. Thus, realizations in the financial statements cannot be reconciled with information announced earlier.

As a result, while information risk has been shown to be priced for large samples of firms, its magnitude for a specific IPO firm is largely unknown at the date of the offering. Thus, investors have to build their IPO pricing on expected values for information risk. The continuous dissemination of information about realized outcomes in the post-issue period enables investors to update their estimates of the firm's information risk. Each newly published piece of information will be judged as either confirmation or revision of earlier announcements and serve to update prior perceptions of quality based on those previously announced pieces of information. This updating process allows investors to gradually replace their expected value with the firm's realized information risk. My hypothesis is that the deviation of expected and realized information risk is associated with the differences in apparent abnormal long-run performance of IPO firms. If the realized information risk is higher (smaller) than the expected information risk, the stock price will correct downward (upward) as the required rate of return is higher (lower), ceteris paribus. The gradual updating process leads to a negative (positive) abnormal return over a lengthy period after the offering.

Several existing empirical publications operationalize information risk with earnings quality metrics, whereby accruals quality (Dechow and Dichev 2002) generally yields the most consistent and robust results (Francis et al. 2004a). However, like other earnings quality metrics in the literature, the estimation of accruals quality requires a long time-series of publicly available accounting data. Such stringent data requirements bias the sample towards bigger and more successful firms. In addition, the calculation of earnings quality over a long trailing time series cannot provide independent firm-year estimations of earnings quality for a given year; thus, changes in earnings quality cannot be fully captured in the year of their occurrence.

These disadvantages of conventional earnings quality metrics make a study of IPO firms' information risk difficult, if not impossible. IPO firms do not have a long historical record of accounting data available, and, by definition, no history of returns data. Furthermore, the study of changes in the information risk of a given firm requires a metric that is able to capture these fundamental changes in a timely manner after the event. In Chapter 3, a short version of the joint work by Ecker et al. (2006), a returns-based metric for earnings quality is developed that satisfies the criteria of a minimized data requirement and independent observations in short time intervals. This measure is the slope coefficient from a firm-specific regression of daily excess returns on a factor mimicking portfolio capturing accruals quality, *AQfactor*, controlling for other factors known to affect returns (market risk premium, size and book-to-market ratio). To assess whether the factor loadings on *AQfactor*, termed e-loadings, truly capture information quality, a variety of tests are designed, in cross section and in time series, for different samples where there are objective indications of variation in information quality such as restatements, lawsuits for accounting allegations and bankruptcies. The construct validity tests show that the e-loadings indeed capture the variation in information quality in the expected way; specifically, e-loadings serve as proxies for firm- and year-specific information risk with a higher (lower) e-loading indicating a higher (lower) information risk.

Chapter 4 addresses the methodological concerns in abnormal return measurement. I reconcile the possibilities of estimating a firm-specific required rate of return and the statistical shortcomings of abnormal return metrics such as the popular buy-and-hold abnormal returns and cumulative abnormal returns. The bottom-line conclusion from this discussion is that the most robust technique to estimate abnormal returns is a calendar-time portfolio approach using an asset pricing model. Most importantly, this method ensures that the cross-correlation in asset returns cannot lead to overstated significance levels for the abnormal return estimates.

My empirical investigation of IPO firms is based on a sample of 6,138 initial public offerings from 1980 to 2002. To connect to prior research in this field, I start by investigating average mispricing for the full sample. The returns of value-weighted portfolios are well explained by the 3-factor asset pricing model, developed by Fama and French (1993), and by the 4-factor asset pricing model, which includes the control for information risk. Equal-weighted calendar-time portfolios, however, show an economically and statistically significant underperformance over the one- and two-year horizons, but not thereafter. Further tests with equal-weighted portfolios show that the underperformance is concentrated in the second year after the issuance. I next modify the calendar-time approach to allow for a more accurate assessment of the persistence of IPO mispricing. Results for rolling 3-months portfolios show that the IPO underperformance does not persist for more than 18-26 months.

The aforementioned tests focus on the *average* firm of the full IPO sample. Turning to the distributional analyses, it is important to note that investors cannot observe the firm-specific sensitivity to information risk at the IPO date. As information risk is priced, however, investors have to form an expectation for the magnitude of this risk. I proxy for the expected value of information risk of IPO firms using the lagged industry average of e-loadings. While no prior IPO research has considered information risk per se, using the industry average information risk as a proxy is consistent with valuation research showing that industry average valuation metrics generally conform to rational expectations.

The ex-post firm-specific e-loading is estimated via an augmented asset pricing regression over the first year[1] of public listing and thus serves as a proxy for information risk in event time. The deviation of the firm-specific information risk from the initially expected information risk serves as the explanatory variable for the abnormal performance of the stock. Positive (negative) deviations indicate that investors initially underestimated (overestimated) the IPO firms' information risk.

The empirical distribution of the 6,138 firm-specific deviations meets the requirement of no systematic error; the median deviation is indistinguishable from zero. Thus, when the sample of IPO firms is split into quartiles, the first two quartiles generally consist of firms with a positive deviation, indicating an initial underestimation of the firm's information risk. Abnormal returns show the hypothesized association with the deviation variable. For example, value-weighted portfolios containing the highest-deviation firms with an initial offering in the last 12 months show an abnormal return of -1.27% ($t = -3.24$) per month over and above the Fama and French (1993) 3-factor model. In contrast, the information riskiness of the lowest (and negative) deviation firms is overestimated at the time of the offering. Portfolios of these lowest-deviation firms show a significant positive return of 1.22% ($t = 3.91$).

So far, I used the 3-factor model to provide results comparable to previous findings in the literature. As information risk is priced, an information risk mimicking factor,

[1] Note that updating the firm's riskiness is assumed to be a gradual process, starting at the date of the offering. Specifically, I do not claim that the e-loading as measured over the first year is 'correct' in the sense that investors do not still place weight on their initial expectations; the updating might still be in progress. On the other hand, the firm-specific e-loading might have fully replaced the lagged industry average earlier than after one year.

AQfactor, should arguably be included in the model for expected returns.[2] The obtained intercept is the abnormal return controlling for information risk. Using this 4-factor model, the difference in abnormal returns of positive and negative deviation firms is slightly more pronounced. In the example from above, firms with worse-than-expected information quality (highest deviation) underperform by −1.47% (t = -3.99), firms with unanticipated good information quality (lowest deviation) outperform by 1.30% (t = 4.23).

Portfolios reflecting longer (2- or 3-year) investments in IPO firms show a marked decline in the magnitude of the abnormal return for both extreme quartiles (although the difference between extreme quartiles remains statistically significant), which leads to the question of how persistent the abnormal performance actually is. Consistent with investors gradually correcting their prior beliefs about the information riskiness, the tests provide evidence for investors and thus the updating becoming more complete, the magnitude of abnormal returns diminishes. I further probe the robustness of results by employing alternative abnormal return metrics, alternative models of market equilibrium, alternative econometric techniques, alternative weighting schemes, and alternative estimation periods for the e-loadings. In all cases, sample partitions based on deviation show that an initial underestimation of the firm-specific information risk maps into underperformance, an initial overestimation into overperformance.

Prior literature and results on the overall sample have concluded that small IPO firms, on average, underperform large IPO firms. Inspection of the size factor loadings for the deviation quartiles in my tests also indicates the existence of a size effect in my sample. To test whether the deviation effect interacts with or is even explained by the size effect, I simultaneously split the sample into deviation and size quartiles. In addition, because small firm effects are isolated, these tests mitigate some of the bad model concerns Fama (1998) raises for small firms. There is generally a monotonic trend within the quartiles of each dimension. For each deviation quartile, the abnormal return declines with size. For each size quartile, I find the hypothesized negative relation between abnormal return and deviation. The differences along the dimensions are as hypothesized and generally significant. Overall, I conclude from these tests that deviation and size effect co-exist and neither dominates the other.

---

[2] Note that in such tests, information risk enters this work in two distinct ways. First, the main analyses of this work are on the distribution (and not on the average) of abnormal IPO returns and therefore require a sample separator. As explained above, I use the deviation of realized firm-specific information risk from the ex-ante expected value of information risk. Second, information risk has been shown to be one determinant of expected returns and, as such, needs to be explicitly accounted for in the asset pricing model in order to fully evaluate abnormal returns.

Switching from a portfolio design to a firm-specific design, I test whether the explanatory power of the deviation is captured by the firm's operating performance. Specifically, I link the abnormal return not only to deviation, but also to the average change in net income over the post-issuance period. As such, I combine potential numerator and denominator effects in a valuation equation. The results show that operating performance is positively associated with abnormal returns: the higher the mean change in earnings, the higher the absolute return. The deviation effect continues to load as expected. Further firm-specific tests show that the significance of the deviation variable is not mitigated by the inclusion of market capitalization and offer volume.

To summarize, even in the absence of an abnormal return for the average firm, there is scope for mispricing. I provide a hypothesis about why some firms should outperform and why others should underperform the benchmark. A combination of both types of firms in one sample lowers the likelihood of finding a mispricing in either direction. At the same time, non-randomly chosen IPO samples might show a spurious abnormal return. On the whole, the results are consistent with an efficient market under information uncertainty where rational Bayesian investors place lower weight on low-quality information. Under this view, the apparent underperformance is just a reflection of rational investor caution when pricing a newly public firm with no information history. As the information risk of a newly listed firm becomes more precisely estimable, the documented mispricings (in both directions) diminish.

The rest of the work is arranged as follows. Chapter 2 provides the valuation framework under information risk. The derivation of the e-loadings and construct validity tests follow in Chapter 3 (this is an abbreviated version of the joint working paper 'A Returns-Based Representation of Earnings Quality' by Frank Ecker, Jennifer Francis, Irene Kim, Per Olsson and Katherine Schipper). In Chapter 4, I first reconcile the debate on abnormal returns measurement in the literature; I then draw conclusions on the methodology to be applied in this study. The chapter concludes with a critical review of existing explanations for abnormal IPO performance followed by the development of my own hypotheses. The main empirical tests follow in Chapter 5, using portfolio designs. Chapter 6 contains the results of firm-specific tests as well as several robustness tests. The work ends with the concluding remarks in Chapter 7.

2. Valuation under Information Risk

Building on prior literature, this chapter discusses the role of information risk in the pricing of stocks. This framework forms the foundation for the main question about how investors price IPO firms. The first section presents two possible definitions of information risk as based on the equilibrium model by Easley and O'Hara (2004). In the second section, different ways of how empirical researchers have operationalized the notion of information risk are presented. The chapter closes with a discussion of the empirical work on information risk and the consequences of information risk for asset pricing and market efficiency.

2.1 Classification of information risk

Each investor's valuation is based on the information set about the firm considered. If and only if the information set is complete and each piece of information is precise, the correct firm value can be inferred. In this traditional framework, by definition, new and relevant information changes investors' estimate of future cash flows and/or the discount rate for these cash flows.

This framework offers two approaches to defining information risk. First, the information set about the firm could be incomplete.[3] Consequently, information risk is the likelihood that a given investor lacks certain pieces of value-relevant information (quantity argument). In other words, there is information asymmetry either between management and market participants or between different groups of investors.

In an equilibrium model of information risk, Easley and O'Hara (2004) consider two groups of investors. The first group has no alternative but to build their investment decisions on public information only; the group member are fully aware that there is second group of investors with additional private information. Informed traders will make use of their informational advantage and hold a different stock portfolio than the uninformed,[4] as they are able to give more weight to stocks with favorable prospects

---

3 The approach here is different to Merton (1987). He assumes some investors are not aware of certain stocks. In contrast, the entire investment opportunities are known in O'Hara (2003) and Easley and O'Hara (2004), but investors lack some pieces of information about specific firms.

4 Note that the uninformed investors have to invest in stocks as only holding the risk-free asset is not an optimal, utility-maximizing investment rule. The utility of investing in stocks for informed traders, however, is higher than for the uninformed.

and less weight to stocks with negative prospects.[5] Uninformed traders therefore are at a disadvantage, and knowing this, will demand a higher risk premium for holding stocks with higher information asymmetry. Stocks with more private information and less public information will, ceteris paribus, have a higher required rate of return. In this view, "firms could lower their cost of capital either by reducing the extent of private information or by increasing its dispersion across traders" (Easley and O'Hara 2004, p. 1572). More relevant information (more disclosure) will reduce the information asymmetry and consequently the risk premium.

Now I focus on the second definition of information risk. The information set might be complete, but the information is potentially imprecise (quality argument). Information risk is then defined as the likelihood of information not accurately capturing the firm's (future) expected cash flows. Following Easley and O'Hara's argument, "the moral hazard problems of self-reporting information may lead the market to be doubtful." In a world of imperfect quality of information, investors will not fully incorporate new information into price. New information can also serve as confirming or correcting signals about prior pieces of information. In other words, new information allows the assessment and revision of the quality of earlier information. Confirming signals do not induce investors to re-estimate future cash flows, but can potentially increase the firm's information quality and therefore lower the discount rate. Correcting signals cause investors to revise their beliefs and can, but do not have to, change the perceived riskiness of cash flows (and one component of the systematic riskiness is information risk).

Easley and O'Hara's model also shows that the firm's cost of capital depend on the precision (quality) of information as the risk of poor information quality cannot be diversified away. Independent of whether the information is public or private, higher information precision leads to lower costs of capital. Lambert et al. (2006) derive the same result. They argue that more precise information facilitates the coordination between the firm and stock holders with respect to capital investment decisions. In equilibrium, the stock market rewards these efforts with a lower cost of capital.

2.2 Empirical measurement of information risk

Easley and O'Hara's (2004) model captures both the quantitative and the qualitative notion of information risk in two separate variables. Lambert et al. (2006) go one step

[5] At the same time, Easley and O'Hara show that stock prices are not able to fully reveal the private information in a dynamic setting.

further and provide analytical evidence that both notions are actually not mutually exclusive, but that it is the average information quality that has pricing consequences, and not information asymmetry per se. Empirical studies, however, have operationalized information risk according to only one definition at a time. Building on the quantitative view, Easley, Hvidkjær, and O'Hara (2002) examine the role of asymmetric information about the firm across investors. They use a firm-specific measure for the probability of information-based trading (PIN, developed by Easley, Kiefer, and O'Hara 1996), and show that this probability is positively associated with asset returns. This finding is consistent with Easley and O'Hara's (2004) prediction that uninformed traders require a higher rate of return when the probability of informed trading is higher.

Turning to the issue of information quality, Easley and O'Hara emphasize the "important role for the accuracy of accounting information in asset pricing." As accounting methods do not change "the firm's underlying business or economic profits," information quality cannot play a role in standard asset pricing models (e.g., the CAPM). Building on such arguments, several existing empirical studies focus on an accounting-based approach and operationalize information risk by using earnings quality metrics.

Prior research has identified accounting earnings as a key piece of information a firm provides to its investors (see, e.g., Francis, Schipper, and Vincent 2003 and Liu, Nissim, and Thomas 2002). In addition to the general importance of earnings to investors, its informativeness about cash flows (as the ultimate determinant of value) can also be used to discriminate between good and bad information quality. Francis et al. (2004a) perform a comparison of different earnings quality metrics used in the literature. Specifically, they compare the relative and incremental explanatory power of earnings persistence, predictability, smoothness, value relevance, timeliness, conservatism, and accruals quality.[6] Single-attribute regressions of the firm's cost of equity capital show both the highest coefficient and the highest Adjusted R^2 for accruals quality. In the multivariate regression including all earnings attributes, accruals quality shows the highest (and most significant) coefficient. In other words, higher earnings persistence or higher smoothness in the earnings series, for example, do not have the same lowering effect on

6 Accruals quality will be presented in detail in the next chapter. Briefly, it is the standard deviation of the error term from a regression of current accruals on cash flows from operations. Earnings persistence is the slope coefficient and predictability is the standard deviation of the error term in a first-order auto-regressive process. Smoothness is the ratio of the standard deviation of earnings over the standard deviation of cash flows. Value relevance is the explanatory power in a regression of returns on earnings and the change in earnings. Timeliness is the explanatory power of a reverse regression of earnings on positive and negative returns. Conservatism is the ratio of the slopes on negative returns over the slope on positive returns. See Francis et al. (2004a) for more details about the operationalization of these earnings quality metrics.

the cost of capital[7] as better accruals quality in the cross-sectional comparison. Based on this work, I argue that accruals quality captures information quality adequately in an empirical sense, and does so more comprehensively than other earnings quality metrics.

Earnings quality, however, is not exogenously given, but can be partially influenced by managerial decisions. In general, information quality is determined by factors that are tied to the firm's business and its environment (innate factors) as well as by factors that are under the discretion of management. Prior research has investigated the different pricing consequences of both components. In short, the pricing effects of information quality driven by innate factors are greater than those that are due to managerial discretion. To understand why, consider the following arguments.

In general, the timing of cash inflows and outflows potentially makes cash flow a biased estimator of the true economic performance in a given period. Therefore, the financial reporting system does not exclusively rely on cash, but also on accruals. The accruals component in earnings reflects cash flows in earlier and later periods which - from a economic point of view - 'belong' to the current period. For example, depreciation expense distributes the cash payment for a machine over its expected lifetime to ensure that proceeds and expenses in individual periods match. While there is evidence that the cash component of earnings is not at the discretion of management (see, e.g., Beneish 1997), accruals can be subdivided into a non-discretionary and a discretionary component. In the example of the machine, the firm has to spread the depreciation expense over its lifetime; that is, the very fact that the firm needs the machine for its production necessitates the accrual (non-discretionary accrual). However, the exact estimation of the expected life of the machine is under (some) managerial discretion, making part of the accrual a 'discretionary' decision variable.

As is intuitively clear from the example, discretionary accruals are based on management assumptions and expectations. Guay, Kothari, and Watts (1996) subdivide discretionary accruals into three components. First, managerial assumptions can be used to reflect management's superior knowledge about the true economic performance of the firm. But second, the discretion over accruals can also be used to smooth the time series of earnings or to avoid the incidence of losses, in order to mask the true economic performance of the firm (so-called opportunistic earnings management). The third component are just errors, i.e. pure noise. The first motivation (reflecting superior knowledge) aims to providing information of higher quality, noise and earnings man-

[7] Francis et al. (2005) extend the finding for expected stock returns to the costs of debt.

agement should lower the firm's information quality. In total, management has some influence on whether they want to provide more or less precise accruals estimates. Francis et al. (2005) examine which motive for exercising discretion over accruals dominates. Specifically, they identify five innate factors[8] to discriminate between non-discretionary and discretionary information quality. In pooled regressions on firm-year observations, innate information quality has a statistically and economically significant relation with the cost of capital in the predicted way. The coefficient on discretionary information quality is also significant, but is much smaller in magnitude than the coefficient on innate information quality. This finding is consistent with discretionary information quality being a mixture of (favorable) performance adjustment on one hand and (impairing) noise and earnings management on the other hand. Importantly, they show that in 58% of their firm-year observations, management uses its discretion to reduce the information risk induced by innate factors.

In sum, financial information is most important to investors. Financial reports of different firms will have differential information quality according to (i) the firm's production technology and business model, and (ii) management's intents. Therefore, it is not a given that information is always precise or just as precise as possible, given the business model.

For the purpose of further empirical analyses in this work, information risk is going to be defined as either the risk of missing some information (lack of quantity of information) or the risk of having imprecise information (lack of quality of information). The pricing effects of the former, while possible to establish statistically, are generally small in economic magnitude.[9] The pricing effects of the latter are generally substantially bigger (Francis et al. 2005), which is why I concentrate on information quality. Derived from the empirical superiority of the accruals quality metric, information risk is the likelihood that firm-specific information is of poor quality, where 'poor' refers to a weak mapping of earnings into previous, present and future cash flows. Sorting it into Easley and O'Hara (2004) terminology, the accruals quality measure captures the precision of public (accounting) information.[10]

---

8 The five factors are the standard deviation of sales and cash flows, the length of the operating cycle, the firm's size and the incidence of losses in the past.

9 See, for example, Botosan (1997), who investigates how the number of disclosures affects a firm's cost of capital.

10 As discussed in Ecker et al. (2006), there are alternative measures of information asymmetry building on market microstructure, specifically the aforementioned PIN scores. However, data limitations preclude their estimation for NASDAQ firms. As a consequence, the metrics are only attainable for NYSE and AMEX firms starting in 1983. In my setting, all IPOs on the NASDAQ market (the majority of firms) would have to be excluded from the sample. Furthermore, Ecker

2.3 Conceptual consequences of the introduction of information risk

The introduction of information risk calls for a more general definition of market efficiency. According to common definitions (see, e.g., Fama 1970), an efficient market fully and immediately incorporates new information into prices. Implicitly, this view is based on the premise that this information is fully credible, i.e., investors trust this new information. The theory as outlined above, however, requires a broader definition of market efficiency in an information risk setting, specifically with regard to the arrival of new information. The more credible a new piece of information, the faster and the more complete it will be incorporated into price. Only new information that is fully certain will be priced instantaneously to the full extent. In contrast, if a new piece of information has low credibility, it will not be immediately and fully incorporated into price; (later) confirming signals are needed to verify the information. Thus, the market needs time to incorporate new and uncertain information. Asset pricing models that ignore the uncertainty in new information can produce spurious abnormal returns over the period during which new information makes it way into price. This spurious anomaly, however, cannot be used to reject market efficiency; it is just a reflection of rational and cautious investor behavior.

Francis, LaFond, Olsson, and Schipper (2004b) examine the role of information risk in explaining previously documented financial anomalies. Specifically, they link, e.g., the post-earnings-announcement drift and value-glamour strategies to the firm-specific information risk and show that information uncertainty is always associated with extreme investment signals. They further document that the initial reaction in the form of short-term abnormal returns is more muted for firms with high information risk than for low information risk firms. Later confirming signals, however, have a greater impact on high-information-risk firms. Comparing the abnormal returns in more detail shows that the (higher) abnormal return for high-risk firms converges to the abnormal return of low-risk firms.

The above findings are consistent with investor rationality under information uncertainty. Specifically, Bayesian theory predicts that investors place less weight on noisier signals; the result is a more muted initial reaction to, for example, the announcement of an earnings surprise, both positive and negative. When subsequent earnings announcements confirm the sustainability of this former extreme earnings figure, two

at al. show that PIN scores, while valid information asymmetry proxies, provide less empirical power.

effects compound. The new information per se is more credible (has a larger impact on price) and the credibility of the former signal is higher, making the price reaction even more pronounced. In the example, the post-earnings-announcement drift can only be established for firms with high information risk, firms with low information risk (and therefore credible announcements) do not show any drift. In sum, whereas the initial reaction on low-risk firms' signals immediately captures the full price impact of the announcement (as market efficiency predicts), high-risk firms' announcements are less credible and require subsequent confirmation. During the period when uncertainty is resolved, the return of high-risk firms 'drifts' toward the return of low-risk firms. This distribution of a pricing effect over a lengthy time period can thus be explained by rational investor caution.

To summarize the empirical evidence, information risk is priced in the capital markets. The empirical and theoretical evidence thus indicates that information risk should be included in the estimation of expected returns. Aboody, Hughes, and Liu (2005), for example, examine the abnormal returns on insider trading and argue that "insiders should earn abnormal returns after controlling for all risk factors, including the systematic component of asymmetric information risk." Consequently, they estimate abnormal returns with a regression including the information risk factor. In the empirical tests of this work, I consider the results incorporating information risk as consistent with prior empirical evidence. For comparability, however, I also present results using the 3-factor model as in Fama and French (1993).

3. Derivation of a Returns-Based Measure of Information Quality

In this chapter, I present the development and validation of a returns-based earnings quality metric, termed e-loading. This chapter is an abbreviated version of Ecker, Francis, Kim, Olsson, and Schipper (2006).[11] In short, e-loading is the firm-specific slope coefficient on an information quality mimicking factor from an asset pricing regression and thus a returns-based representation of the perceived information quality.

There are two main reasons why e-loadings are superior to the existing metrics in the literature and make the study of information risk in an IPO setting feasible. First, e-loadings can be calculated for a comprehensive sample of firms and do not require a time-series of accounting data. The latter is simply not attainable for IPO firms. Second, e-loadings can be adjusted to measure information quality in event time. Changes in information quality can therefore be measured in a timely manner. In contrast, traditional earnings quality metrics are calculated over a certain and usually lengthy time period. For example, the calculation of accruals quality is over seven years at a minimum. When a change from one period to the other occurs, only the last of the seven annual observations actually reflects this change in earnings quality. Thus, traditional earnings quality metrics behave like slow moving averages and are not able to immediately indicate changes. For a metric to be less static, the frequency of independent observations must be higher. Independent accruals quality observations can only be assessed every seven years, requiring fourteen consecutive years of accounting data.

Accruals quality – the underlying construct of e-loadings – goes back to Dechow and Dichev (2002). It is the standard deviation from a regression of current accruals on past, present and future cash flows from operations. The intuition for this measure is as follows. The evaluation of current accruals only requires cash flow data with one lead and one lag term, as the operating cycle of most firms is below one year. Thus, there is no empirical justification why present current accruals should persist for longer than one year. Conversely, cash deferrals in the prior year should map into the present year's earnings.[12] On the whole, current accruals in the present year should map into

[11] The validity test presented here are of particular relevance to highlight the advantageousness of this metric for this work. The interested reader is directed to Ecker et al. (2006) for additional tests, all of which show consistent results with respect to the construct validity.

[12] See Dechow and Dichev (2002), who derive this relation in a formal model.

cash flows from operations in the last, the present or the next year. If this mapping is not accurate, an error will occur capturing the portion of current accruals which does not correspond to a cash flow in the adjacent fiscal years. But to the extent that this error in accruals is constant and therefore predictable, investors can learn from past observations and will not perceive this error as a 'risk', independent from its sign and magnitude. It would simply be an indication of a bias in current accruals. What should be perceived as risk is its variability. Consequently, the accruals quality metric is the standard deviation over error terms from consecutive years. Besides the three cash flows, McNichols (2002) adds the two explanatory variables, taken from the modified Jones (1991) model. The basis model is transformed into a model of current accruals being explained by past, present and future cash flows from operations, as well as the change in sales and the gross property, plant and equipment. From a purely econometric standpoint, this adjustment increases the model's explanatory power. Intuitively, the change in sales is intended to control for growth effects, the inclusion of property, plant and equipment controls for differences due to the firm's capital intensity, which may be correlated with size.

In the first step, the relation of current accruals and cash flows from operations is most conveniently captured by a regression. Whereas Dechow and Dichev (2002) use a rolling time window of seven years, a cross-sectional form of this regression on the industry level is employed here for the following reason. To the extent that all firms in a given industry face the same business environment and therefore have similar capabilities to estimate current accruals, the regression would not show any error term for a given firm. If a positive (negative) error occurs, the firm's accruals are too high (low) to be explained by the cash flows from operations, after normalizing for industry effects. The 48 industries are defined using the Fama and French (1997) classification scheme. In the second step, five (firm-specific) error terms are then required to calculate the (firm-specific) standard deviation. To abstract from their magnitude (and make results comparable across firms), all variables in the regression and therefore the error term and its standard deviation are scaled by average assets in fiscal year T.

$$
\begin{aligned}
CurAcc_{j,T} &= \phi_{0,j} + \phi_{1,j} CFO_{j,T-1} + \phi_{2,j} CFO_{j,T} + \phi_{3,j} CFO_{j,T+1} \\
&\quad + \phi_{4,j} \Delta Rev_{j,T} + \phi_{5,j} PPE_{j,T} + \upsilon_{j,T} \qquad (1)
\end{aligned}
$$

$$
\begin{aligned}
CurAcc_{j,T} &= \Delta CA_{j,T} - \Delta CL_{j,T} - \Delta Cash_{j,T} + \Delta STDEBT_{j,T} \\
&= \text{firm j's current accruals in year } T; \\
CFO_{j,T} &= NIBE_{j,T} - TA_{j,T} \\
&= \text{firm j's cash flow from operations in year } T;
\end{aligned}
$$

$$
\begin{aligned}
NIBE_{j,T} &= \text{firm j's net income before extraordinary items} \\
&\quad (\textit{Compustat} \ \# \ 18) \text{ in year } T; \\
TA_{j,T} &= (\Delta CA_{j,T} - \Delta CL_{j,T} - \Delta Cash_{j,T} + \Delta STDEBT_{j,T}) - DEPN_{j,T} \\
&= \text{firm j's total accruals in year } T; \\
\Delta CA_{j,T} &= \text{firm j's change in current assets } (\textit{Compustat} \ \# \ 4) \\
&\quad \text{between year } T-1 \text{ and year } T; \\
\Delta CL_{j,T} &= \text{firm j's change in current liabilities } (\textit{Compustat} \ \# \ 5) \\
&\quad \text{between year } T-1 \text{ and year } T; \\
\Delta Cash_{j,T} &= \text{firm j's change in cash } (\textit{Compustat} \ \# \ 1) \\
&\quad \text{between year } T-1 \text{ and year } T; \\
\Delta STDEBT_{j,T} &= \text{firm j's change in debt in current liabilities } (\textit{Compustat} \ \# \ 34) \\
&\quad \text{between year } T-1 \text{ and year } T; \\
DEPN_{j,T} &= \text{firm j's depreciation and amortization expense} \\
&\quad (\textit{Compustat} \ \# \ 14) \text{ in year } T; \\
\Delta Rev_{j,T} &= \text{firm j's change in revenues } (\textit{Compustat} \ \# \ 12) \\
&\quad \text{between year } T-1 \text{ and year } T; \\
PPE_{j,T} &= \text{firm j's gross value of property, plant and equipment} \\
&\quad (\textit{Compustat} \ \# \ 7) \text{ in year } T.
\end{aligned}
$$

For each firm-year with the necessary data, regression (1) is estimated over a minimum of twenty firms in a given industry. These estimations yield firm- and year-specific residuals, $\hat{v}_{j,T}$. For each year, this step is repeated for all industries and firms with the necessary data. Requiring five residuals for consecutive years leads to a time-series of $\hat{v}_{j,T}$ for the years $T-5$ to $T-1$. The standard deviation of these five residuals of firm j is the accounting-based accruals quality metric $AQ_{j,T}$.[13] Calculating the $AQ_{j,T}$ measure using the residuals in years *T-5* to *T-1* accounts for the fact that Equation (1) contains a lead term, $CFO_{j,T+1}$. For this reason, there is no requirement of foreknowledge about cash flow data to estimate the AQ metric in any given year. Large (small) values of $AQ_{j,T}$ correspond to poor (good) accruals quality.

A potential criticism about this measure is that it is only able to reflect the quality of current accruals ignoring any long-term accruals component. This concern is refuted

[13] Note that switching from the time-series design of Dechow and Dichev (2002) to the cross-sectional design does not lower the data requirement for the sample of AQ firms. The need for five consecutive firm-specific error terms to calculate the standard deviation is equivalent to the need for a seven year-window in Dechow and Dichev. In contrast, the additional requirement of twenty firms in a given industry raises the bar for whole industries to be included.

by Ecker, Francis, Olsson, and Schipper (2005). Specifically, Ecker et al. extend the Dechow-Dichev measure to the more comprehensive notion of total accruals quality. Replacing current accruals with total accruals as dependent variable also requires a new definition of the cash flow measure. Similar to current accruals mapping into cash flows from operations, total accruals should map into free cash flows to the unlevered firm. As these figures contain flow figures beyond the operating cycle (such as depreciation, most prominently), the additional question arises of how many leads and lags are to be included in the regression. Using different procedures, Ecker et al. (2005) estimate optimal lead-lag structures for each industry. The total accruals measure is the standard deviation of the error terms from a regression of free cash flows of several leads and lags on total accruals. Having estimated the total accruals quality for a matched sample of firms[14], the authors perform a correlations analysis and show that current accruals quality is indeed a valid proxy for total accruals quality.

Each firm with at least one AQ estimate is assigned to an AQ decile using a dynamic portfolio technique that allows for differences in firms' fiscal year ends as well as over-time changes in accruals quality. Specifically, deciles are formed on the first day of each month m based on the firm's most recent value of AQ known prior to m; firms with the smallest (largest) AQ values are placed in the first (tenth) decile. The AQ metric is assumed to be known by the stock market three months after the firm's fiscal year end. This means that firm j's AQ signal for fiscal year T, where fiscal year T ends in month n, will influence firm j's ranking for months $n+4$ through $n+15$. In a next step, the average daily return for each decile is calculated, starting on January 2, 1970 (the first trading day of 1970) to December 31, 2003. This yields a time series of 8,586 daily returns for each decile. The AQ-factor-mimicking portfolio, $AQfactor$, equals the difference between the daily returns of the four poorest-AQ deciles and the four best-AQ deciles. This procedure, similar to that used by Fama and French (1993) to construct size and book-to-market factor-mimicking portfolios, and in particular to that by Carhart (1997) to construct the returns momentum factor, yields a series of 8,586 daily $AQfactor$ returns ($AQfactor_t$).

For this time period, the average value of $AQfactor_t$ is 0.0779%, or about 22% on an annualized basis. The average daily excess market return is 0.0216%, the average value of the daily Fama-French size factor *SMB* is 0.0021% and the average value of the daily Fama-French book-to-market factor *HML* is 0.0224%. $AQfactor$ is reliably different from zero (t = 9.17) and has a higher t-statistic than the other risk factors (the t-

[14] The data requirement of total accruals quality is much more stringent than for current accruals quality because of the extended lead-lag structure of the free cash flows. Therefore, the sample of total accruals quality firms is a subset of the current accruals quality firms.

statistics for market risk, *SMB* and *HML* are 2.12, 0.37 and 4.28, respectively). Because *AQfactor* is time-specific and not firm-specific, it is possible to correlate *AQfactor* with the returns of *any* firm to determine that firm's exposure to poor earnings quality, similar to the correlation of a firm's returns with the market risk premium to obtain a measure of its exposure to market risk (beta). The specific (partial) correlation measure is the coefficient estimate on *AQfactor* obtained from an augmented 3-factor asset pricing regression which includes *AQfactor* as an additional independent variable. This coefficient estimate on *AQfactor*, e-loading, reflects the market evaluation of accruals quality, over the known risk factors included in this model:

$$\begin{aligned} R_{j,t} - R_{F,t} &= \alpha_{j,T} + \beta_{j,T}(R_{M,t} - R_{F,t}) + s_{j,T}SMB_t + h_{j,T}HML_t \\ &\quad + e_{j,T}AQfactor_i + \epsilon_{j,t} \end{aligned} \tag{2}$$

The subscript t denotes the trading days in year T; $R_{j,t}$ = firm j's return on day t; $R_{F,t}$ = the risk free rate on day t; $R_{M,t}$ = the market return on day t; SMB_t = small-minus-big factor on day t; HML_t high-minus-low book-to-market factor on day t. [15] $e_{j,T}$ is the estimate of firm j's sensitivity to poor earnings quality in year T. The other slope coefficients have similar interpretations, capturing the exposure to returns representations of market risk, size, and book-to market, respectively, in year T. Note that while the market factor is the value-weighted return of all securities in the CRSP universe (Amex, NYSE, NASDAQ), the other three factors *SMB*, *HML* and *AQfactor* represent the returns on zero-investment portfolios which are consistently long in the stocks that have empirically been shown to earn, ceteris paribus, a higher return and short in the stock of the opposite characteristics that are shown to earn a lower return. For example, *HML* is the return on a portfolio which is long in high-BM stocks and short in low-BM stocks.[16]

In summary, the procedure creates an accounting-based measure of accruals quality $AQ_{j,T}$ using a restricted sample of firms with seven consecutive years of accounting data available, converts AQ to a time-specific returns representation ($AQfactor_t$), and then uses this time-specific returns representation in firm- and year-specific regressions to obtain a firm- and year-specific e-loadings. Relative to the underlying accounting-based measure, e-loadings can be calculated for much larger samples, because they require only enough daily returns in year T to estimate the asset pricing regression. In addition, *AQfactor* varies through time with a daily frequency, meaning that the

---

15 The data for the market factor, *SMB* and *HML* is obtained from Kenneth French's website. http://mba.tuck.dartmouth.edu/pages/faculty/ken.french/data_library.html.

16 For details on the factor construction, see Fama and French (1993).

Table 1: Descriptive statistics for selected financial variables

The data for market value, total assets and sales are in millions.

AQ Sample

	Mean	Std. dev.	10%	25%	Median	75%	90%
Market value	1,294.97	4,938.84	7.97	24.95	114.08	617.69	2,539.33
Total assets	1,403.51	4,123.69	15.53	43.90	170.94	800.05	3,137.31
Sales	1,298.30	3,451.51	16.99	53.93	210.98	872.37	3,109.41
ROA	0.037	0.086	-0.043	0.015	0.046	0.078	0.114
ROE	0.073	0.183	-0.106	0.035	0.105	0.157	0.213

Returns Sample

	Mean	Std. dev.	10%	25%	Median	75%	90%
Market value	942.49	4,133.90	6.01	17.44	72.41	375.47	1,588.85
Total assets	1,004.68	3,488.89	10.19	27.51	98.75	443.31	1,985.70
Sales	907.51	2,874.54	9.60	30.40	114.79	483.29	1,896.36
ROA	0.026	0.106	-0.078	0.008	0.044	0.078	0.118
ROE	0.055	0.208	-0.179	0.019	0.100	0.156	0.218

firm-specific e-loading as the regression coefficient is allowed to vary from year to year. Stated differently, the e-loading is not constrained to be slowly changing, as is AQ which requires seven years of data and therefore has a mechanical dependence year over year.

To illustrate the importance of the sample bias, two samples of firms are formed. The AQ Sample consists of all firms with the necessary data to estimate AQ in each year T=1970 – 2003; all firms with at least 100 daily returns in year T are included in the Returns Sample. As expected, the number of firms in the Returns Sample is much more comprehensive with a mean of 6,408 firms per year versus 2,147 firms per year in the AQ Sample. The respective means correspond to 92.4% vs. 30.9% of all publicly traded firms with data on CRSP. Table 1 reports summary information about the distributions of size (market capitalization, total assets and sales) and performance (return on assets (ROA) and return on equity (ROE)) for the two samples. The comparison between the AQ Sample and the Returns Sample shows that the former contains larger and more successful firms. These descriptive data demonstrate that the Returns Sample dominates the AQ Sample in sample size and has less survivorship bias. As the Returns Sample only requires 100 daily returns per year, it is more representative of the population of traded firms than the AQ Sample, which requires a time-series of seven years of accounting data for inclusion in any yearly sample.

E-loadings also offer the advantage of independent observations in a high frequency. Therefore, changes in earnings quality have the computational possibility of immediately mapping into changes in the earnings quality metric. This flexibility is arguably best shown for situations with objective indications of poor earnings quality. Three such settings are considered next: restatements, shareholder lawsuits because of accounting violations and bankruptcy.

Three event samples are formed and firm-specific e-loadings for all firms in the samples are calculated. The restatement sample contains 788 firm-year observations with the necessary data from the General Accounting Office's study on Financial Statement Restatements, which covers January 1, 1997, through June 30, 2002. Data on class action securities litigation over the period January 1, 1990, through April 24, 2003, are from Woodruff-Sawyer Co. and from the Securities Class Action Clearinghouse. The data requirements reduce the final lawsuit sample to 793 observations. The bankruptcy sample consists of 618 firms that went bankrupt during 1970 to 2003 as indicated by the delisting codes obtained from CRSP. Requiring sufficient returns data to estimate e-loadings for a given year yields to 371 observations.

The benchmark for the e-loadings comparison is constructed by randomly selecting 100 non-event samples with the same number of firms as the corresponding event sample. To control for over-time changes in information quality in the overall population, e-loadings are selected from all non-event firms such that each random sample has the same year-by-year distribution as the corresponding event sample. The mean e-loading of the event sample can be conveniently compared to the mean e-loading of the 100 non-event samples. The variance of the individual e-loadings in the event sample and the variance of the mean e-loadings of the 100 non-event samples are used to calculate the (parametric) test statistics on this difference.[17] In a non-parametric test, the mean e-loading of the event sample is ranked within the distribution of 100 mean e-loadings of the non-event samples. For example, a percentile rank of 100 implies that the event sample e-loading is the largest e-loading value of the complete distribution of mean e-loadings for the random non-event samples.

[17] The calculation of the test statistics assumes independence between event sample and non-event sample estimates. To the extent this assumption is violated, assuming independence will overstate the variance of the difference and lead to more conservative test statistics.

If e-loadings truly reflect real changes in earnings quality, one would expect each event sample to have a larger e-loading than the non-event samples in the year of the event, denoted 'Year 0'. More importantly for the illustration of its flexibility, the average event sample e-loading should increase over time, relative to the e-loadings of comparison non-event samples, with a peak of the difference in the year of the event.

Table 2 displays the findings starting in the fifth calendar year prior to the event until Year +1. (By definition, the analysis of the bankruptcy sample ends in Year 0.) Across all panels, the hypothesized behavior of the metric is found. The mean e-loading of the 'restatement sample' in Panel A is strictly increasing from Year -5 onwards and is highest in Year 0. This is consistent with investors perceiving the firm's information quality as deteriorating and therefore demanding a higher risk premium for this firm. To some extent, the increase of e-loadings might just be a reflection of over-time changes in the population earnings quality, as indicated by the benchmark of the non-event samples.[18] More weight should therefore be placed on the analysis of the difference instead of the change in e-loadings over the years. The difference is insignificant for the four years prior to the event, indicating that the monotonic pattern is largely due to a general decrease in earnings quality. In Year 0, however, the difference in e-loadings of 0.1081 indicates a measurable deterioration in earnings quality. After the restatement, in Year +1, the e-loading is still high compared to the non-event samples, but decreases somewhat. This indicates that information quality is improving, but the firm's credibility after a restatement is still low in a cross-sectional comparison (difference of 0.0730, t = 2.22). The non-parametric test on the difference reveals the same qualitative picture. Starting at an insignificant level in the center of the distribution, the e-loadings for the restatement sample are higher than all random sample means in Year 0 and Year +1.

Panel B shows the results for the lawsuit sample. The average firm that is to be sued for accounting violations is actually of good earnings quality as indicated by the t-statistics and the percentile ranks for the difference in early pre-event years. Only in Year +1, the earnings quality of event sample and non-event sample are of comparable magnitude. In the years of and following the event, the average e-loading is highest for the event sample with a highly significant difference of 0.1142. Assuming that the average *AQfactor* over this sample period (January 1990 to April 2003), 13.84%, is representative for each year in the sample period, this difference translates into an average annual expected return premium of 1.58 percentage points for event firms compared

18 As noted earlier, its construction assures that the benchmark accounts for over-time effects. This is of particular relevance as the average e-loadings for the population can be expected to increase over time.

to non-event firms. For the lawsuit sample, the difference does not decline, but even increases from Year 0 to Year +1.

The sudden deterioration of earnings quality for the lawsuit sample indicates that investors are rather surprised at the time of the event. Quite contrary, e-loadings for the bankruptcy sample in Panel C are already high in the fifth year before the event; the difference from non-event firms is significant at the 1% level ($t = 2.86$). This is consistent with prior research that documents the ability of investors to recognize the signs of financial distress early. Among others, Altman (1968) already examines a discriminant analysis to predict bankruptcies using financial ratios. The difference in e-loadings is highest in the year of bankruptcy.

Taken altogether, these tests provide evidence that e-loadings are able to capture changes in earnings quality in a timely manner. This characteristic is essential for the research question of this work. I use an average e-loading as expected value for the information risk of the IPO firm at the date of the issuance. After the listing, investors will gradually update their prior belief with the firm's true riskiness. Naturally, the examination of this process requires a metric that is able to reconcile this change. In addition, the minimum requirement of only 100 trading days can easily be met by most IPO firms. Third, the usage of the time-specific *AQfactor* assures that e-loadings can be calculated in event time rather than calendar time.

Table 2: Comparison of e-Loadings of Event Firms with Non-Event Firms

The 'restatement sample' contains 788 firms in the years 1997 to 2002; the 'lawsuit sample' consists of 793 firms that were alleged accounting violations from 1990 to 2002. The 'bankruptcy sample' contains 371 firms that went bankrupt from 1970 to 2003. The columns labeled "event sample" show the mean e-loading for all event firms in year $T = -5, +1$ (for the bankruptcy sample: $T = -5, 0$). The columns labeled "non-event sample" show the average e-loading calculated across the 100 non-event samples. The columns labeled "Diff." show the difference between the mean values of the e-loadings for the event and non-event samples; the columns labeled "t-stat". show the t-statistic for the difference being distinguishable from zero. Finally, the columns labeled "%-tile" show the percentile rank of the mean e-loading of the event sample within the empirical distribution of 100 mean e-loadings for the non-event samples.

Panel A: Restatement Sample

	Event Sample	Non-Event Sample	Diff.	t-stat.	%-tile
Year -5	0.1018	0.1292	-0.0274	-0.76	18
Year -4	0.1116	0.1433	-0.0317	-0.98	10
Year -3	0.1321	0.1521	-0.0200	-0.68	20
Year -2	0.1591	0.1636	-0.0045	-0.17	42
Year -1	0.1951	0.1902	0.0049	0.18	58
Year 0	0.3153	0.2072	0.1081	3.57	100
Year +1	0.2694	0.1963	0.0730	2.22	100

Panel B: Lawsuit Sample

	Event Sample	Non-Event Sample	Diff.	t-stat.	%-tile
Year -5	0.0280	0.1277	-0.0996	-2.61	1
Year -4	0.0653	0.1265	-0.0613	-1.74	3
Year -3	0.0313	0.1266	-0.0953	-2.98	1
Year -2	0.0917	0.1433	-0.0516	-1.73	3
Year -1	0.1573	0.1552	0.0021	0.08	60
Year 0	0.2773	0.1631	0.1142	3.48	100
Year +1	0.2857	0.1519	0.1338	3.74	100

Panel C: Bankruptcy Sample

	Event Sample	Non-Event Sample	Diff.	t-stat.	%-tile
Year -5	0.2428	0.1135	0.1293	2.86	99
Year -4	0.2431	0.1092	0.1340	3.15	100
Year -3	0.2748	0.1177	0.1571	3.90	100
Year -2	0.3478	0.1284	0.2194	5.33	100
Year -1	0.5158	0.1365	0.3793	7.74	100
Year 0	0.5154	0.1265	0.3888	4.06	100

4. Abnormal Returns Measurement and Hypotheses Development

4.1 Methodological issues in long-term abnormal returns measurement

Abnormal stock returns are in the focus of many different research questions. There is, however, an extensive debate in the literature on how abnormal returns should be estimated. This section critically reviews this debate and provides a rationale for the approach as applied in this work. A reader whose interest in methodological issues is limited might want to continue with Section 4.2. In short, the approach used in this work is a calendar-time approach where monthly expected portfolio returns are described by an asset pricing model.

4.1.1 What return is normal?

Prior literature concentrated on IPO underperformance only, but the arguments in this section also apply to abnormal return measurement in general, positive or negative. The literature on abnormal IPO performance started with Ritter (1991) who found a significant underperformance relative to the benchmark. The result directly contradicts short-run studies that provide evidence that IPO stocks outperform on the day of their initial listing. Thus, the general belief of IPO stocks being underpriced is just a (very) short-run phenomenon. More importantly, the trading strategy based on the observable fact of an initial offering (buying the benchmark and selling the IPO firm) promises abnormal returns over several years on a zero-investment portfolio. For this reason, Ritter rejects the hypothesis of market efficiency.

Since then, many articles on long-term abnormal return measurement have been published, both with direct reference to new listings and more generic methodological articles that use simulations to support their argumentations. Unfortunately, the authors do not agree on a single methodology, and results are highly sensitive to the method applied. Fama (1998) argues that most of the abnormal return anomalies documented by prior literature cannot constitute justification for rejecting the null hypothesis of no abnormal return. As overreaction is as frequent as underreaction and no consistent theory is able to explain both, these apparent deviations from market efficiency cancel out. The methodology used by the anomalies' authors is subject to an extensive debate in the literature. There are three main critiques. First, the benchmark for determining what return is expected (normal) is false (i.e., a bad model problem). As abnormal returns can only be evaluated jointly with the model for expected returns and the bad model is unavoidable, this claim can always be raised. Therefore, the task is to minimize, not to eliminate the impact of the bad model problem. The two general approaches to defining expected returns, matching and asset pricing model, are discussed in this subsection. Second, there is a debate about the period over which the event firm and benchmark returns are measured, as described in the following subsection. Third, there are concerns with the validity of statistical inferences as significance levels may be biased, outlined in Subsection 4.1.3. This methodological section concludes with a summary of the analysis and a discussion of the remaining methodological issues in Subsection 4.1.4.

All methods for measuring and evaluating abnormal returns have advantages and disadvantages. The researcher's task is to find the method that is least likely to overstate the results or to introduce bias. Along with the empirical findings in the new offerings literature, this chapter discusses the pros and cons for each method. Due to the recommended caution, the baseline conclusion is to apply one of the most robust techniques leading to conservative rather than overstated results.

Matching technique

Extracting an abnormal part from ex post stock returns requires a definition of normal or expected returns as a benchmark for this stock. There are two basic approaches to solving this problem. Normal returns could be defined by comparing returns of event firms with those of non-event firms, or by an asset pricing model, such as the CAPM by Sharpe (1964) and Lintner (1965) or the Fama and French (1993) 3-factor model. I start by describing the former method, the so-called matching technique.

Event firms' performance can be compared to ('matched to') another non-event firm or a portfolio of non-event firms with similar characteristics known to affect expected returns. The underlying idea is that the benchmarks capture firm-specific characteristics potentially explaining risk differentials. Ideally, matching is not only able to control for cross-sectional differences in expected returns, but also for coincidental sample-specific patterns in average returns (see Fama 1998). Measuring abnormal returns as the deviation from matched firms' returns has the advantage of implicitly allowing for changes in the risk sensitivities of event firms over time. However, the approach is only valid as long as one assumes that shifts in the riskiness affect the event firm and the matched firm similarly. There will be no indication of an abnormal return if an economic shock affects the return of both groups in a similar way. In contrast, the technique produces spurious abnormal returns when the external shock has a different impact on event and benchmark firms, raising the question of whether the matching technique really controls for all necessary risk exposures.

Following Banz (1981) finding that small firms (in terms of market capitalization) have a higher expected return than big firms, even after controlling for differences in their market risk sensitivity (the CAPM beta), it was popular to choose comparable firms on the basis of size only. After Fama and French's (1992, 1993) work on the book-to-market ratio (henceforth: BM) as a determinant of cross-sectional differences in average returns, the technique has been refined to pick comparables from the pool of similar size and BM firms.

In an IPO setting, it is not recommended to match firms only by size. This is because the group of low-market-capitalization firms in the population also consists of long-term losers and distressed firms, undoubtedly having different characteristics than IPO firms. As Brav and Gompers (1997) emphasize, IPO firms are low-BM firms whereas long-term losers generally show high-BM. Partially, this concern is alleviated when matching is based on both size and BM. Brav and Gompers (1997) apply this improved matching technique and refute the Ritter (1991) and Loughran and Ritter (1995) result of a significant abnormal return when only size is controlled for.

The matching technique is not sensitive to the selection criteria only, but also to the pool of non-event firms from which matches are chosen. Brav and Gompers (1997) and Brav et al. (2000) find no difference between event and non-event firms when matching on BM and size, leading them to conclude that any underperformance is a general pattern in small and low-BM firms' returns rather than an issuance effect. But this finding is also subject to debate. Loughran and Ritter (2000) argue that the similarity in expected returns reflects a bias in the CRSP sample. Brav and Gompers (1997) and Brav (2000) do not require each benchmark firm to survive the whole five-year period over which they measure abnormal returns. Omitting this filtering procedure, they include 200-300 small new bank listings per year with very low returns. These issues are not contained in the standard IPO databases and therefore not filtered out. This leads to an underestimation of their abnormal returns metric of about one percent per year. Loughran and Ritter (2000) directly address this issue by forming zero-investment portfolios of issuing and non-issuing firms. They document a significant return difference over all size and BM groups once the small bank listings are excluded.

Barber and Lyon (1997) conclude that matching firms by size and BM leads to unbiased estimates and alleviates three potential biases in sampling situations. The research design works well in random samples as well as in samples with either a size-based or a BM-based sampling bias. However, Barber and Lyon only examine extreme size and extreme BM deciles separately. No inferences can be drawn on how the matching technique would work for samples where both a size and a BM bias prevail as is the case with an IPO sample. Additionally, as Mitchell and Stafford (2000) point out, major corporate financing events are not at all random, but a self-selected sample. For samples with severe biases, Kothari and Warner (1997) document a higher likelihood of finding both a significantly positive or a significantly negative abnormal return, depending on sample characteristics. Therefore, Kothari and Warner conclude that it is "difficult to generalize about whether the results for a particular study are driven by an overrejection bias or whether they occur in spite of an underrejection bias."

Barber and Lyon (1997) highlight another potential problem. When randomly drawing firms by size, the probability of picking a smaller firm depends on the size of the event firm. In an IPO setting with mainly small firms, for example, the likelihood of picking bigger firms with, ceteris paribus, lower expected returns is higher. Thus, estimations would be systematically biased to find a positive abnormal return and at least understate an existing negative abnormal return.

Spiess and Affleck-Graves (1995) also cast doubt on the validity of the matching approach. They argue that matched firms are likely to be used several times when several matching criteria are applied. Thus, the benchmark for event firms is repeatedly used to determine an abnormal return. This leads to a bias in test statistics as observations cannot be considered independent. On the other hand, the restriction of simply using each matching firm only once limits the ability of the technique to mimic the essential risk characteristics of event firms. This is of particular relevance in an IPO setting where small and low-BM firms dominate the sample. Matches would likely be biased towards bigger and higher BM firms, as generally no lower categories exist.

Eckbo, Masulis, and Norli (2000) argue that apparent issuer underperformance is just a reflection of a lower systematic risk exposure relative to the matching firms. Specifically, they compare size- and BM-matched firms and SEO firms by forming a zero-investment portfolio which is long in matched firms and short in issuers. If matching truly accounts for all risk differences, this portfolio should not load on any factor in an asset pricing regression. A significant loading on the market factor, however, shows that the matching technique solely based on firm size and BM misses the differential market sensitivity (i.e., the difference in betas). Due to this difference, the expected returns for matched and event firms are different, leading to spurious abnormal returns. Differences in betas of IPOs and matched firms are also documented by Ritter (1991), although he only uses size as matching criterion. Using a simulation approach, Lyon, Barber, and Tsai (1999) also confirm that controlling for size and BM is not sufficient for unbiased inferences from nonrandom samples (like IPOs).

Asset pricing model

The second way to determine a normal return is to use an asset pricing model. Traditional implementations of the CAPM describe the cross-section of returns simply as the firm's exposure to the overall stock market defined as the value-weighted market index less the risk-free rate. The higher the firm's loading on the broad market, the higher the expected return. Theoretically, normal returns should be based on a normative theory such as the CAPM. Unfortunately, neither betas of the single-period CAPM nor the consumption betas of the intertemporal CAPM by Breeden (1979) have significant empirical power to explain cross-sectional differences in stock returns (Fama and French, 1993).

Fama and French (1992) provide evidence that both the firms' size (market value of equity) and the BM have high explanatory power for returns. In their 1993 article, they augment the CAPM by the returns of two zero-investment portfolios mimicking the size and the BM risk. Consistent with the empirical result of small firms having a higher return, they capture the size risk with a portfolio of buying small stocks and selling big stocks (*SMB*). The second zero-investment portfolio is long in high-BM stocks and short in low-BM stocks (*HML*). The significant factor loadings support their view that the risk differential between small and big firms and low- and high-BM is of interest to the marginal investor and therefore priced. The slope coefficients or loadings on these factors in a time-series regression capture, similar to the loading on the market factor, the firm's sensitivity to the respective factor.

The choice of size and BM as additional risk factors is only at a first glance ad hoc. Fama and French (1995) justify this choice by relating both variables to the firm's profitability. Specifically, they show that a low BM (high market value relative to its book value) is associated with persistently good earnings performance. Conversely, they provide evidence that firms with high BM and thus high positive loadings on the HML factor are firms under relative financial distress. The expected return for low-BM is therefore lower than for high-BM firms. Small firms suffered from a long poor-earnings phase during the 80s. Big firms, however, recovered from the depression in the early 80s more quickly and were no longer affected by this phenomenon, but actually profited from the boom. Although unexplained by fundamentals, this finding points towards the higher riskiness of small firms requiring a higher compensation; hence, size is negatively correlated with stock returns. Studies that extend the estimation period over the Fama-French horizon show that this phenomenon has reverted in more recent years. The average SMB factor is statistically indistinguishable from zero (0.12% per month, $t = 0.60$)[19] over the sample period from 1980 to 2003. Nevertheless, the size factor continues to have significant explanatory power for returns.

Up to the mid-nineties, a stream of literature about 'anomalies' in stock returns for which the CAPM cannot offer an explanation emerged. Fama and French (1996a) use the 3-factor model to explain many of the previously documented anomalies. The most prominent examples are the size effect by Banz (1981) and the BM effect first documented by Stattman (1980) which are simply captured by differential loadings on the respective factor. Abnormal returns have also been shown to be associated with extreme earnings/price ratios, cash flow/price ratios and sales growth (see, e.g., Lakonishok, Shleifer, and Vishny 1994). Typically, these firms load heavily on the HML factor. Consistent with the relative distress hypothesis, firms with extremely low values load positively, firms with high values load negatively on the HML factor. Both the SMB and the HML factors are needed to empirically capture the long-term return reversal phenomenon documented by DeBondt and Thaler (1985).

For my purposes, there are at least three reasons for applying a multi-factor model for stock returns besides consistency with prior literature. First, the CAPM suffers from very low power in explaining the cross-section of stock returns. Most prominently, Fama and French (1992) show that the basic prediction of the CAPM does not hold for their sample: Stock returns are not positively associated with market risk exposure as captured by their beta. Second, the abnormal returns estimation would be biased towards finding only risk differentials when the sample is biased in one or more omitted risk dimensions. A third justification might be derived from the empirical success of the 3-factor model. For the stock portfolios under examination in the Fama and French (1993) article, the augmented regression leads to abnormal returns generally indistinguishable from zero and Adjusted R^2s of close to one.

Loughran and Ritter (2000) argue against using a positive (only based on empirical findings) theory as established with the Fama-French multi-factor model as these tests are not able to reject market efficiency, but are just tests if an anomaly is explained by other factors included in the asset pricing regression. Instead, tests of market efficiency should be based on an equilibrium (normative) model. Fama and French (1996a), in

19 Data is obtained from Kenneth French's website
http://mba.tuck.dartmouth.edu/pages/faculty/ken.french/data_library.html.

contrast, claim that the 3-factor model could indeed be viewed as an equilibrium model, if size and BM are proxying for two state variables investors care about. Fama (1996) shows that the 3-factor model is consistent with the more general intertemporal CAPM (Merton 1973) and the arbitrage pricing theory (Ross 1976). His result provides a justification that their positive model using a market, size and BM factor is close to an equilibrium pricing model in which size and BM are at least valid proxies for state variables.[20]

But as previously noted for the matching technique, the asset pricing model approach is also not without shortcomings. Fama and French (1993) show that using mimicking factors goes along with a limited ability of the model to account for the *complete* cross section of average returns. The significant intercepts of a time-series regression indicate that the 3-factor model is unable to fully capture the returns of 25 portfolios, formed from size and BM quintiles. Specifically, the results indicate that the model has difficulties in explaining the size effect in the lowest-BM portfolios. The smallest firms have a significantly negative abnormal return, the biggest low-BM firms have a positive abnormal return. In sum, as Fama (1998) and Mitchell and Stafford (2000) point out, the 3-factor model cannot even fully explain the return differences along the dimensions it is designed to account for.

Several authors have tried to improve on the explanatory power by adding or redesigning factors. Brav, Geczy, and Gompers (2000) replace the original HML factor with a similar factor only containing small firms. They justify their approach with the Loughran (1997) argument that mainly small Nasdaq and Amex firms are responsible for the explanatory power of BM. Eckbo et al. (2000) employ a six-factor asset pricing model based on macroeconomic risks. Both approaches fail to explain the return of the smallest-/lowest-BM portfolio. In addition, the 3-factor model cannot capture the short-term performance continuation documented by Jegadeesh and Titman (1993), the so-called returns momentum. By identifying short-term winners, it is possible to earn a positive abnormal return over the 3-factor model. For this reason, Carhart (1997) developed a momentum factor as the zero-investment portfolio long in last year's best performers and short in last years' worst performers.

---

20 This view of the 3-factor model as a rational pricing model is not without criticism. Fama and French (1996a,b) provide a discussion on the main critiques: Lakonishok et al. (1994), Haugen (1995) and MacKinlay (1995) emphasize that there is an irrationally high risk premium for firms under financial distress and that it is this irrationality that prevents the 3-factor model from collapsing into the CAPM. Second, Kothari, Shanken, and Sloan (1995) consider the Fama-French results for equally-weighted portfolio returns as outcomes of a survivorship bias in the Compustat database. The latter concern is directly rejected by Chan, Jegadeesh, and Lakonishok (1995) who find that survivorship bias is not severe. Using a sample free of this bias, they are able to show that low BM stocks outperform. Fama and French (1996b) argue in a similar fashion.

Compared to the matching approach, an asset pricing model has the advantage that out-of-sample estimations can be avoided. No pre-event observations are required to estimate a normal return. Equivalently, there is no need for a non-event sample, which is particularly useful in event studies where the matched firm is also potentially influenced.[21] Brav and Gompers (1997) motivate the use of the 3-factor model with the possibility for convenient statistical inferences. With the underlying assumption of multivariate normality of the residuals, inferences on abnormal returns can be drawn similar to Jensen's alpha in the CAPM (Jensen 1969). This is not possible when the distribution of abnormal returns is skewed, as is the case with buy-and-hold abnormal returns, for example.

Both approaches, matching and asset pricing model, only offer an incomplete description of a normal return and have difficulties in explaining the returns of the smallest firms. Brav et al. (2000) emphasize that model misspecification can never be rejected offering the possibility for supporters of market efficiency to claim that a significant abnormal performance is due to incorrect measurement of normal performance. Fama (1998) argues that size and BM alone are clearly not capturing all differences in returns; Eckbo et al. (2000) agree and provide evidence that matching ignores the market factor in expected returns. Thus, the matched firm technique is at least as prone to the bad model problem as an asset pricing model. Also, there is no theoretical framework whether one should match firms by industry, size, BM, or by any combination of the three. Different matching methods can lead to very different results. In my view, these two reasons outweigh the criticisms against asset pricing models, hence I will apply the 3-factor model in the following analyses.

Whether one views the 3-factor model as a close-to-accurate description of an equilibrium or 'just' a positive theory, it is widely used in the literature. I want my results to be comparable to earlier work which mainly documents the ability of the 3-factor model to explain the cross-section of returns in several different settings. Further, caution recommends setting the hurdle for establishing an abnormal return high. I would argue that a new issue puzzle totally explained by the 3-factor model would not be a puzzle, but just a size and BM effect. This argument clearly outweighs the concern by Loughran and Ritter (2000) against positive asset pricing theories.

---

21 According to Ritter (1991)'s supply response hypothesis (to be discussed in more detail later), managers are able to time the IPO such that they can make use of a temporary overvaluation of stocks. If this hypothesis is correct, the pool of potential matched firms is also mispriced, making a significant spread less likely. Additionally, the degree of overvaluation might be different for more mature firms and the overpricing might resolve in a different speed.

As outlined in the chapter on the valuation framework, information risk is priced and should therefore be included in the estimation of expected returns (i.e., in the asset pricing model). I assess the influence of different benchmarks on the main results by augmenting the asset pricing model with the AQ-mimicking factor, $AQfactor$.[22] The analysis above also indicates that both the matching technique and asset pricing models have difficulties in explaining average returns of small stocks. The concern of small firms driving the result is addressed in three ways. First, the main results are presented using value-weighted portfolios. Second, an additional ranking on size is performed and third, the sensitivity of the results is assessed by separately deleting the smallest firm-months observations.

4.1.2 Choosing the right metric

There are three metrics in studies of long-term performance: buy-and-hold abnormal returns (BHARs), cumulative abnormal returns (CARs) and average abnormal returns (AARs).[23] Ritter (1991) uses abnormal returns on a buy-and-hold strategy in his first study of long-run IPO performance. Starting at the time of the event, monthly returns are compounded to a return for the following months:

$$BHAR_{i,T} = \prod_{t=1}^{T}(1 + r_{i,t}) - \prod_{t=1}^{T}(1 + E[r_{i,t}]) \tag{3}$$

$r_{i,t}$ is the return of the event firm i in month t. Common values for the period T are 36 to 60 months.[24] As Fama (1998) discusses there is no asset pricing model for returns over three or more years, so the expected return on a long-term buy-and-hold strategy, E[$r_{i,t}$], must be modeled by a benchmark of matched firms. The mean $BHAR_T$ over a sample of event firms can be calculated as equal- or value-weighted average of the individual $BHAR_{i,T}$.

In general, the use of a single firm as a benchmark for long-term returns is problematic. The likelihood of idiosyncratic factors emerging during the returns estimation

---

22 In a sensitivity test, I generalize the findings to also hold using the CAPM model.

23 In the next subsection, I additionally introduce the abnormal returns estimated by a calendar-time portfolio approach. Because of the similarity in the derivation and the statistical properties, the intercepts in a calendar-time approach could be viewed as a variant of AARs.

24 Firms delisted during the return estimation period are commonly included in the sample. For example, in Ritter (1991), the average life of an IPO firm is only 34 months when calculating 36-months BHARs.

period is increasing in the horizon. These firm-specific factors could dominate the estimation of normal returns reducing the abnormal return calculation to a lottery. In an IPO setting, the matched firms are implicitly required to be listed before the event firm's offering and therefore introduce a potential survivor bias. Thus, single firms as benchmarks have to be ruled out leaving portfolios as benchmark for buy-and-hold returns.

While all metrics are usually based on monthly returns, steps are ordered differently in the CAR and AAR calculations, relative to the BHAR calculation. First, the abnormal returns are estimated on a monthly basis and then the abnormal return over the (full) horizon of interest is calculated. The cumulative (average) abnormal return is the sum (average) of month-specific abnormal returns. The expected return $E[r_{i,t}]$ can be proxied by a matched portfolio (a value- or equal-weighted market index, or a size- and BM-matched portfolio) or a matched firm. As, unlike in the calculation of BHARs, abnormal returns are calculated on a monthly basis, asset pricing models are also alternative proxies for the expected return.

$$CAR_{i,T} = \sum_{t=1}^{T} r_{i,t} - E[r_{i,t}] \tag{4}$$

$$AAR_{i,T} = \frac{1}{T} \sum_{t=1}^{T} -E[r_{i,t}] \tag{5}$$

Similar to the discussion concerning the choice of the benchmark in the previous section, there is no consensus in the literature about the right metric for a long-term performance study. The null hypothesis of such a study is commonly that there is no abnormal performance over a certain period of months. In view of their supporters, this hypothesis demands the use of BHARs over the very same period. On a theoretical level, Barber and Lyon (1997) and Lyon, Barber, and Tsai (1999) conceptually favor buy-and-hold abnormal returns because they accurately mimic investors' returns (or "experience"). CARs do not reflect the abnormal returns for an investor buying the event firms and shorting the benchmark over the full horizon. Mitchell and Stafford (2000) relax this argument by pointing out that buy-and-hold is only one of the possible investment strategies. It is also reasonable to assume an investor who performs a monthly portfolio rebalancing as necessary to mimic CARs or AARs.

As significant abnormal returns are used to reject market efficiency, Fama (1998) argues that the return metric has to be the one invoked by the asset pricing model.

There are simply no models for expected returns over several years. Most commonly, asset pricing models are tested on monthly data.

Mitchell and Stafford (2000) add to this debate that BHARs give a false impression on the adjustment speed. Abnormal returns appear to persist over a long period, although they may only occur for a much shorter time. Even worse, Mitchell and Stafford argue that BHARs increase with an increase in the horizon under consideration. To see this, consider the following example, taken from Fama (1998): The event firm (the benchmark) has a 10% (0%) return in the first year after the event. In the years 2 and 3, both rise by 200%. This corresponds to a 3-year BHAR of 20% for the event firm (1.1 x 2 - 2). If only one year had been considered, the BHAR would have been 10% only. Thus, the abnormal return estimation increases, although there is no return difference between event firm and benchmark after the first year. As this horizon cannot be derived from theory but is chosen arbitrarily by the researchers, it is impossible to infer from the analysis of BHARs over different holding periods how long an abnormal return actually persists.

Starting from the perspective that BHAR is the right metric, Barber and Lyon (1997) provide evidence that CARs are biased estimators of BHARs. In particular, when calculated using a reference portfolio such as a market index, CARs are seriously affected by a new listings bias. This bias occurs because newly listed firms are typically included in the benchmark, whereas the firms in the event sample generally have a long returns history. As a result, significance levels of CARs are overstated. In an IPO setting, this concern is likely of marginal importance. Event firms do not have a long history by definition. Including (later) IPOs in the benchmark would only lower the power of detecting an abnormal return, thus biasing the results in favor of the null hypothesis. Loughran and Ritter (2000) use this argument for their claim that the Fama-French model has low power to detect an abnormal return in an offering setting as the factors themselves are "contaminated" with new listings. New issues thus serve as part of the benchmark for their own return, effectively diminishing the spread. However, this concern has been shown empirically to be of no influence of the results. Eckbo et al. (2000) and Brav et al. (2000) change the factor construction such that no issuing firm return is included. Intercepts and R^2s of the asset pricing regression are only marginally affected. In contrast to the biases in CARs, Barber and Lyon (1997) further argue that BHARs are mostly affected by the periodic rebalancing of benchmark portfolios. This bias arises because the benchmark portfolio (such as the market index or another matched portfolio) changes its composition when firms list and delist whereas the composition of the event portfolio remains constant.

In addition, statistical inferences from asset pricing models rely on normally distributed returns. The normality assumption is a better approximation for shorter return intervals, such as a month. Fama (1998) emphasizes that the distributional properties and test statistics of AARs or CARs are simply better understood. It is well documented in the literature (see, e.g., Mitchell and Stafford 2000 and Brav 2000) that the distribution of firm-specific $BHAR_{i,T}$ is skewed to the right and is generally not centered at zero. The right skewness of BHARs makes statistical inferences more difficult, and the use of common test statistics is impossible. Barber and Lyon (1997) and Kothari and Warner (1997) simulate the influence of BHARs skewness on common statistical inferences. According to Mitchell and Stafford (2000), the skewness problem is decreasing in sample size. The assumption of normality is a better approximation for large than for small samples. Still, sample size can only partially mitigate, not eliminate the concern.

A solution to the skewness problem is provided by the bootstrapping procedure as first applied in this context by Brock, Lakonishok, and LeBaron (1992) and Ikenberry, Lakonishok, and Vermaelen (1995). Bootstrapping provides an empirical distribution under the null hypotheses of no abnormal return. The underlying assumption is that the expected return can be proxied by the average return of the sampled distribution, often sampled from the pool of firms with similar size and BM as the event firms. Ikenberry et al. (1995) match each event firm to a non-event firm in the same size and BM portfolio at the date of the event. The result is a pseudo sample of firms with the same event date, size and BM distribution. This step is repeated many times, often a thousand times. The average BHARs of the resulting 1,000 pseudo samples form the distribution with mean and variance under the null hypotheses. The significance of the difference between the event sample average and the distribution mean can be assessed using the empirically generated distribution.

A compelling reason against the use of BHARs is the unavoidable bad model problem. Every asset pricing model is an incomplete description of the cross-section of returns. Consequently, bad model problems cannot be avoided and the reproach of misspecification cannot be rejected. With the extension of the return measurement over several years, the likelihood of such a misspecification increases due to the compounding pricing errors induced by model misspecification. However, even when monthly data is used to calculate a cumulative abnormal return, Conrad and Kaul (1993) cast doubts on the CAR method inducing spurious biases. Specifically, they criticize that CARs in event-time studies can bias the results in either direction because of bid-ask-spread bounces. They show in detail that the thereby induced measurement error in monthly abnormal returns is compounded when computing long-term CARs with the overall bias increasing in horizon length. In contrast, when calculating AARs, there can be no compounding of errors. If errors are sufficiently random across months, they would even cancel out. In sum, AARs are preferred because they are calculated with monthly data and avoid compounding potential misspecifications of the asset pricing model. I continue in the next section by showing that the abnormal returns from a calendar-time portfolio approach share this property and can conceptually be considered a variant of AARs.

4.1.3 Event-time vs. calendar-time approaches

Lyon et al. (1999) develop a method for BHAR estimation robust to the new listings bias, the rebalancing bias and the skewness problem. They advocate the use of benchmarks that simply do not suffer from new listings and are not rebalanced. The skewness problem is mitigated by a skewness-adjusted test statistic. Despite their progress in controlling for three potential biases, their method cannot control for the severe problem of cross-sectional dependence in returns.

Mitchell and Stafford (2000) criticize that the typical BHAR falls far in the tails or even outside the null distribution. The common advice to employ a 'carefully constructed benchmark' has then little impact on the inference for large samples. When event BHARs are far below the distribution minimum of non-event BHARs, their p-value remains unchanged at 0%, no matter what benchmark is used. Mitchell and Stafford conclude that the bootstrapped distribution, designed to solve the skewness problem, is too tight to allow reliable inferences. Bootstrapping requires the independence of observations. BHARs, however, are measured in event time (i.e., each IPO is an observation) leading to correlated observations. Lyon et al. (1999) define three potential sources for this dependence in abnormal returns: average return overlapping, calendar clustering and industry clustering.

Average returns overlap arises when the first offering of the firm is followed by a second offering by the same firm within the period over which the abnormal return for the first offering is measured. For example, estimating a 3-year BHAR return for two offerings that only differ by a year would produce an overlap of 24 monthly returns, i.e. the exact same 24 observations go into both BHAR estimations. By definition, this (most severe) dependence problem cannot arise in a study of IPOs as each firm has only one event.

Calendar clustering and industry clustering also introduce dependence in the form of cross-correlation. There is evidence that initial offerings (and corporate events in general) cluster in time and by industry (see, Mitchell and Stafford 2000 and Brav 2000). Thus, return periods of firms within the same industry are likely to overlap. When return periods overlap, even in the case of different firms, total independence is no longer a given. For example, macroeconomic (industry) factors will influence all (several) firms' returns at a specific point in time. The influence is likely to be of different magnitude for different firms, but yet contemporaneous returns are correlated across firms. For example, Bernard (1987) shows an average correlation of market-adjusted returns of 23% across firms. The cross-correlation concern is likely to be even more pronounced for a sample of IPOs. Those firms are not only clustered by industry, but also of similar size and in a similar stage of the life cycle.

Intuitively, the dependence problem increases in sample size and BHAR horizon. All else equal, the likelihood of overlapping estimation periods increases with the number of events (observations) in a given sample period. Similarly, the longer the return estimation period, the higher will be the likelihood of another event being in this period. The positive dependence in long-term abnormal returns will not lead to biases in the estimated coefficients, but ignoring a positive covariance systematically understates the variance of (bootstrapped) distributions of BHARs. The diminished variance maps directly into higher parametric test statistics, which therefore may be overstated.

Brav (2000) develops a Bayesian technique designed to correct inferences from BHARs for dependence and skewness. Fama (1998) and Mitchell and Stafford (2000) both emphasize that Brav's methodology is limited to certain circumstances (e.g., industry clustering) and mitigates but does not eliminate the dependence problem. In addition, Fama (1998) points out that the applicability of Brav's approach is limited as the "number of return covariances to be estimated is generally greater than the number of time-series observations."

Both Brav (2000) and Mitchell and Stafford (2000) show that accounting for dependence has a large effect on test statistics. Mitchell and Stafford directly compare the bootstrapping procedure of Ikenberry et al. (1995) assuming independence and their own procedure controlling for cross-correlation. Whereas the former method leads to significant results, none of the three samples considered still shows a significant abnormal return when dependence is accounted for. They stress the fact that their results are not dependent on the benchmark construction, but solely to the control for dependence. For this reason, Mitchell and Stafford generally question the validity of statistical inference based on bootstrapping methodologies.

BHARs are calculated over the full horizon of interest and cannot be broken down to specific (calendar) months. As such, BHARs are always event-time abnormal returns with one event being one observation. The obtained average of the individual BHARs is the return on the strategy of investing an equal amount in each IPO firm. In contrast, calendar-time approaches weight each month equally mimicking the strategy of investing in an event-firms *portfolio* each month. The firm- and month-specific abnormal returns that form the basis for the CAR and AAR calculation can also be used to form a monthly portfolio of event firms.[25] The two metrics themselves, however, are cumulated or averaged, respectively, on a firm-by-firm level, which categorizes them into the event time metrics (also with each IPO being one observation). Intercepts of a calendar-time portfolio regression resemble AARs in that they also yield per-month abnormal return estimations. In addition, both approaches 'average' over monthly observations allowing for model misspecifications for individual months to cancel each other out.

Forming a portfolio of event firms for a given month is the most robust method to control for cross-sectional dependence. The return horizon (equals the investment horizon for a specific stock) is 'outsourced' into the portfolio formation rule. Suppose one wants to examine three-year returns after an offering. For each month with returns data available, a portfolio of firms with an IPO in the last 36 months is formed. Going forward in time, firms are dropped in month 37 after the event, newly public firms are included in the portfolio, and so on. Thus, this approach corresponds to an investment strategy with monthly (at least periodic) portfolio rebalancing. The result is a time-series of portfolio returns that automatically accounts for cross-correlation (because no inference is based on cross-sectional standard errors). Building on the results discussed in the previous section, the Fama-French asset pricing model serves as benchmark. The regression intercept is the estimate for the abnormal return on this investment strategy. This approach is applied by Mitchell and Stafford (2000) and Hou, Olsson, and Robinson (2001). Even Lyon et al. (1999) admit the superiority of calendar-month portfolios when sample returns are correlated due to estimation period overlap or industry clustering. Loughran and Ritter (2000) argue that calendar month approaches are likely to understate the abnormal return when underperformance is clustered in months with many events. The reason is that not an event, but an event *month* is treated as one observation. Mitchell and Stafford (2000) refute this concern by showing that there is no difference in abnormal performance between months of many and few issuances.

[25] As discussed in the next section, the noise in daily returns data hampers the reliability of estimating month-specific abnormal returns with an asset pricing model.

4.1.4 Concluding remarks and problems discussion

To summarize the preceding section, the most robust tests are based on a calendar-time portfolio approach using monthly data. Using monthly data avoids the skewness problem and forming portfolios completely accounts for the cross-correlation problem. Statistical inferences can conveniently be drawn from the time-series of portfolio returns. One counterargument is that only long-term buy-and-hold returns mimic investor experience; however, buy-and-hold is only one of many investment strategies. Another strategy with periodic portfolio rebalancing is also a long-term investment in IPO firms.

The structure of the IPO portfolio could follow either equal- or value-weighting. Prior literature has well established that abnormal performance disappears or shrinks substantially when value-weighted portfolios are employed (see, e.g., Brav and Gompers 1997 and Mitchell and Stafford 2000). Loughran and Ritter (1995) and Brav and Gompers (1997) draw inferences from 3-factor regressions on the time-series of monthly average returns, the method also used in this study. They all show insignificant value-weighted abnormal returns, but significantly negative abnormal returns for equal-weighted portfolios.

Fama (1998) uses this differential finding to conclude that underperformance is restricted to tiny firms in the sample and recommends putting more weight on the value-weighted portfolio results. He argues that not only is the total wealth effect for investors captured in the appropriate way, but also is the bad model problem less of a concern (as all asset pricing models including the 3-factor model have problems in capturing the complete size effect when applied to the smallest firms (see, e.g., Fama and French 1993). As equal-weighting puts more weight on small firms, the likelihood of an apparent underperformance only induced by the method is higher. However, Brav et al. (2000) add to this discussion that equal-weighted portfolios should be used if the researcher is interested in the implications of potential stock market mispricing for managerial decision making.

Loughran and Ritter (2000) doubt the validity of value-weighted portfolios in detecting underperformance. Assuming that percentage mispricing is higher for small than for big firms, the value-weighted portfolios are forced to show a less negative (and possibly a non-significant) underperformance. Their argument builds on the wider bid-ask-spreads of small firms. Higher transaction costs, arising from lower trading liquidity, make it harder for traders to exploit an obvious mispricing. A second concern is that value-weighted portfolios have the largest standard errors of all their specifications. They argue that the higher standard errors are partially attributable to few dominating firms in the portfolios. The unsystematic risk cannot be diversified away when only small firms complete the portfolio composition. In contrast, naïve diversification by equal-weighting would reduce idiosyncratic risk (Fama 1976).

Note that an equal-weighted portfolio strategy requires monthly rebalancing even when the number of firms in the portfolio and their number of outstanding shares remain unchanged. Different returns for the firms change the market capitalizations which need to be (re-) standardized to one to serve weights for the following month. In this study, I do not limit the analysis to one weighting scheme throughout the work and leave this decision to the reader. Only when the overall economic relevance of IPO mispricing should be assessed, I favor the value-weighted portfolio results, for the simple reason that bigger firms tend to be of higher importance.

Articles using a calendar-time portfolio approach to measure abnormal performance of IPO firms are relatively rare. Earlier papers generally apply a different methodology, recent papers focus on other corporate financing events. Mitchell and Stafford (2000), for example, provide evidence for the case of seasoned equity offering (SEO) firms. Brav et al. (2000) present results for equal- and value-weighted portfolios from 1975 to 1992 using the Fama-French model as benchmark. The portfolio contains IPO firms not listed for more than five years. They only find significant underperformance for the equal-weighted portfolio of -0.37% (t = -1.94) per month. Deeper investigation shows that this abnormal return is concentrated in the smallest tercile of firms in their sample (-0.65%, $t = -2.29$). The same research design is applied by Ritter and Welch (2002). For equal-weighed calendar-time portfolios from 1973 to 2001, they find no significant underperformance (-0.21%, $t = -1.23$). Only when they place higher weight to the burst of the internet bubble in 2000, the intercept is significantly negative with -0.48% ($t = -2.01$) per month. Although insignificant for the whole period, they interpret their results supportive for the relative underperformance of IPO firms.

The calendar-time portfolio approach, however, is also not free of limitations. In a regression on the complete time-series of IPO portfolio returns, one assumes the factor loadings to be constant over the sample period. However, as Mitchell and Stafford (2000) point out, this may not be true as the portfolio composition changes through time. Specifically, IPOs tend to cluster by industry. At the same time, firms in different industries have more pronounced differences in risk sensitivities than firms within a given industry. As firms drop out and other firms are included in the portfolio, the assumption of constant portfolio risk sensitivities might therefore be too stringent. This concern is first partially addressed when the sample is split into subperiods. More directly, this concern is mitigated by a variant of the calendar-time portfolio approach, as presented in detail and applied in Section 6.1.

In short, the difference between the methods lies in the order of steps to be taken. Whereas the main method uses simple monthly returns to form a portfolio, the alternative method estimates month- and firm-specific abnormal returns before forming portfolios.[26] This method, discussed by Fama (1998), estimates the abnormal monthly returns on a firm-by-firm basis, so the individual loadings vary across firms. With changes in the portfolio composition, the implicit loadings to estimate the mean abnormal return in a given month also change.

Calendar-time portfolios contain a varying number of firms. As the portfolio variance is, all else equal, a decreasing function of the number of firms in the portfolio, it is likely that the variance of the regression residuals also changes through time. The point estimate would still be unbiased, i.e. the estimate would converge towards the true population value with increasing sample size, but it is no longer efficient. It does not have the minimum variance within the class of all unbiased estimates (see Gujarati 2003 for a detailed problem description). One potential control would be a weighted least squares estimation with weights proportional to the square root of the number of firms included. Mitchell and Stafford (2000) reject this possibility by showing that, in essence, the weighting scheme will weight each event equally and undo the whole reason of forming calendar portfolios in the first place, namely the correction for cross-correlation. Jaffe (1974) and Mandelker (1974) standardize the monthly abnormal portfolio return by the standard deviation of individual abnormal returns (as a measure of precision) which are only attainable when the alternative method of the calendar-time approach (Jaffe-Mandelker method in the sensitivity section) is used.

Hou et al. (2001) propose another solution to this problem. They use a generalized, autoregressive, conditional heteroscedasticity model (GARCH 1,1) to explicitly model the time-varying variance of the regression residual. Specifically, their technique maximizes the joint likelihood of the following two equations:

$$R_t - R_{F,t} = \alpha + \beta(r_{M,t} - r_{F,t}) + sSMB_t + hHML_t + \epsilon_t \tag{6a}$$

$$\sigma^2_{\epsilon,t} = \gamma_0 + \gamma_1\sigma^2_{\epsilon,t-1} + \gamma_2\epsilon^2_{t-1} + \gamma_3 n_t \tag{6b}$$

The residuals ϵ_t are normally distributed with zero mean and time-varying variance $\sigma^2_{\epsilon,t}$. As restrictions on the coefficients apply, the GARCH approach models a large (small)

26 The procedure resembles the calculation of AARs. But whereas AARs are the firm-specific averages over a certain number of months after the event, calendar-time portfolios are formed in advance and then the averages are calculated over the complete time-series of calendar months in the sample period.

absolute value of t and a large variance $\sigma^2_{\epsilon,t}$ mapping into a large (small) variance $E[\sigma^2_{\epsilon,t+1}]$ and thus makes extreme observation in the next period more likely.[27] Note that the model by Hou et al. deviates from a standard GARCH (1,1) model in that the residual variance is also a linear function of the number of firms in the portfolio (n_t). This not only allows for a time-varying variance, but also for changes in point estimates of the first equation, including the intercept.

Mitchell and Stafford (2000) rely on their portfolio creation rule of at least 10 firms in any given month. They find that this requirement alone controls for much of the heteroscedasticity effects. Given this evidence and the difficulties in specifying the order of the GARCH model, I perform both ordinary least squares and the GARCH (1,1) model, but consider OLS as the main approach.

4.2 Explaining abnormal IPO performance

Given Ritter's (1991) evidence that IPO stocks underperform in the long run, the literature is limited to explaining apparent underperformance. However, my hypothesis does not rely on the existence of an abnormal performance on average. In fact, there is no abnormal performance for the full sample of this study (Section 5.2). Thus, I examine to what extent the arguments, originally designed to explain underperformance only, could explain the entire cross section of abnormal returns, independent of whether the distribution is centered at zero or below. The approaches fall into two categories: Schultz (2001), Eckbo and Norli (2005), and Benninga, Helmantel, and Sarig (2005) offer explanations consistent with rational investor behavior. In contrast, Ritter (1991), Morris (1996), and Teoh et al. (1998) deliver behavioral arguments, partially building on investor irrationality, for why IPO stocks underperform.

The explanation by Schultz (2001) is founded on large groups of IPOs following only one or few successful IPOs, consistent with the Loughran and Ritter (2000) finding of underperformance clustering in times of much IPO activity. It relies on the assumption that the large groups of IPOs underperform on average and that they are indeed a large fraction of the sample, relative to the few successful firms that ignited an IPO boom phase. Schultz's argument, however, only applies when IPOs are weighted equally, for example, when BHARs are used. In contrast, calendar-time portfolio approaches weight each month of the sample period equally, independent of the number of IPOs in the portfolio. Thus, it cannot explain the finding of underperformance for equal-weighted calendar-time portfolios.

---

[27] Details can be reviewed in Tsay (2002).

Both, Eckbo and Norli (2005) and Benninga et al. (2005) argue that IPO firms have lower risk. Eckbo and Norli link IPO underperformance to trading liquidity. They show that calendar-time portfolios of IPO firms load significantly more negative on the liquidity factor than portfolios of seasoned firms and infer from this test that IPOs have lower expected returns. This conclusion for the average IPO, however, is only valid if the average factor is distinguishable from zero. Eckbo and Norli's Table 9, however, shows an average factor return of 0.175% per month with a t-statistic of 1.16. Further, they do not establish that there is underperformance in their sample relative to the 3-factor model that would justify the need for a trading liquidity factor as additional explanatory variable. While the former argument casts doubt on the relative explanatory power of trading liquidity for the difference between newly listed and seasoned firms, the latter generally questions the need for trading liquidity in this setting.

Benninga et al. (2005) hypothesize that IPO firms have lower risk because the option to re-privatize is a larger portion of value than it is the case with seasoned firms and that the value of this option has a negative correlation to the overall economy. This value, however, is hard, if not impossible to estimate for a given firm. Further, the holders of the option to go private are the shareholders. Thus, there is no re-privatization if shareholders do not want to hold unlisted stock or are not offered a sufficient compensation for their shares by those who do. Benninga et al. estimate that re-privatization of IPO firms has a likelihood of about 5.2%.

Building on Miller (1977) ideas, Morris (1996) argues that in a world of heterogeneous beliefs and short selling constraints, it is always the most optimistic investors who hold the stock as they are prepared to pay the highest price. In the time after the initial offering, the divergence of beliefs is expected to shrink because investors learn as more information about the firm becomes publicly available. The divergence can only shrink when a) the average investors raise their valuation by a higher amount than the optimistic investors or b) when the optimistic investors lower their valuation by a higher amount than the average investors. Although Ritter and Welch (2002) count the learning explanation to the group of 'semi-rational' explanations, I argue that it is essentially a behavioral argument and can only be justified by irrational investors who in fact do not learn from experience with prior IPOs, neither from own losses nor from just the observation of IPO stock prices.

There are two distinct 'pure' behavioral theories in the IPO literature. Ritter (1991) explains the underperformance of IPO stocks with investor overoptimism (supply response hypothesis). In his view, investors simply overestimate the probability of buying an outperforming IPO stock (such as Microsoft) and pay a higher price for the issue. In the aftermarket, more and more investors, disappointed by the performance, sell their stocks, leading to the underperformance. For this hypothesis to work, additional assumptions for the supply side of IPOs have to hold. First, owners/managers can assess that their issuance will raise more money than the fair value of the stocks should be. Second, they have the ability to time the issuance accordingly.

The first assumption implies managers' knowledge of future stock market performance. Managers have to foresee that the overpricing is only a temporary phenomenon and values will soon revert to their fair level. If stock values are expected to increase further in the future, they would rationally postpone the issuance. This point is criticized by Schultz (2003). He shows that the underperformance of IPOs is only an ex-post phenomenon. His pseudo market timing hypothesis says that IPOs are simply more likely when stock prices increase and that managers have no ability to time the issue because future stock performance is unknown. Even when managers cannot estimate future performance and cannot time the IPO, his simulations reveal that the increasing number of issuance in a bullish stock market is a sufficient condition for subsequent underperformance. Again, this underperformance explanation only works for event-time abnormal returns. As in his earlier article, calendar-time approaches are robust to this concern because they treat monthly portfolios as observations, independent of the number of event firms in this portfolio. The hereby reduced weight for periods with many events makes the underperformance essentially disappear. Eckbo et al. (2000) doubt the validity of Ritter's second assumption. They show that there are no significant differences between the underperformance of utilities firms and the underperformance in other industries. To the extent that the regulation of the utilities industry is a hurdle in timing any issue activity, exploiting such opportunity windows of severe overpricing should yield a different abnormal performance.

The study of Teoh et al. (1998) is related to my study. They start with the premise that there is a high information asymmetry between investors and issuers at the time of the offering. Investors are thus forced to rely heavily on the data in the prospectus containing one to three years of financial statements. Teoh et al. examine disaggregate earnings in the IPO period and find that discretionary accruals are abnormally high. In their view, managers use their discretion to boost earnings which in turn justify a higher IPO price. The modified version of the Jones (1991) model[28] is used to separate the discretionary from the non-discretionary portion. Assuming that the change in sales is the sole determinant for current accruals and gross property, plant and equipment is the sole determinant for long-term accruals, they are further able to form subcategories

---

[28] The approach is taken from Teoh, Wong, and Rao (1998).

for the respective non-current and current accruals portion. Sorted by the amount of abnormal discretionary current accruals (DCA), firms in the 'aggressive' quartile significantly underperform firms in the 'conservative' quartile. They argue that DCA are particularly subject to earnings management. Management has the opportunity and the incentive to boost pre-event earnings by manipulating DCA to arrive at a higher issue price. As information is gradually revealed over time by media, analysts, and financial statements, investors start realizing that earnings are not consistently high, but managed before and during the IPO period. The explanation builds on the marginal investor not rationally discounting for earnings management in forming expectations about future cash flows.

Aside from the exclusive use of event-time metrics and the hereby induced bias in test statistics (discussed in Section 4.1.3), I identify several further issues with Teoh et al. (1998)'s study. I consider it unlikely that current accruals at the IPO date determine the stock performance over several years because the operating cycle for most firms is below one year.[29] Consistent with this criticism, but directly contradicting their main hypothesis, their regression analysis shows that there is no explanatory power of initial DCA (taken from the first post-issue statements) for returns in months 18 to 29 after the IPO. They ascribe the null finding to noise.

Perhaps the main concern, however, is that the Teoh et al. (1998) explanation excludes investor learning. Despite large differences in the DCA across quartiles, the conservative half of the sample does not show any significant abnormal performance. That is, according to the Teoh et al. figures, an investment in an IPO is at best a zero NPV investment (if investors are able to detect and avoid abnormal DCA firms), and on average a negative NPV investment (if investors are unable to detect abnormal DCA). In a repeated scenario (such as the IPO market), investors would learn these facts. The learning argument finds some support in the analysis of sample periods. In the first subperiod, all DCA quartiles indicate a significant underperformance, regardless of the metric used. In the second subperiod, however, only the coefficient for the most aggressive quartile, and only when CARs are used to assess abnormal returns, is still significant, in spite of a 51% increase in the number of observations and the associated increase in statistical power. In addition, the magnitude of the point estimate is cut in half. This finding is arguably more consistent with a learning story than with a continuous fooling story.

---

29 For example, Francis et al. (2004a) report that only 10% of all firms in their sample have operating cycles of more than 236 days.

The behavioral (or 'semi-rational') explanations in the literature, referenced above, rely on at least some degree of investor irrationality. It is not that investors are unable to see that managers time IPOs strategically or that they are unable to distinguish sustainable earnings from a temporarily inflated earnings figure. But investors do not learn from their mistakes that cost money in the past. Further, several empirical studies (referenced in the previous section) have found that underperformance is not a general phenomenon. The evidence that there is, on average, no abnormal performance allows for the possibility that some firms underperform and other firms outperform. Underperformance explanations therefore miss a sizeable portion of the cross-sectional distribution of post-IPO performance.

I offer (and test) an alternative explanation for apparent IPO mispricing, building on rational investor behavior with respect to information uncertainty. Investors are unable to estimate the firm's information risk at the offering date and have to rely on an expected value. With the continuous dissemination of new information, investors are able to gradually replace their prior belief with the firm's true information risk. If the prior was an underestimation of the riskiness and the expected returns is thus too low, the stock price should decline and show a negative abnormal performance. If, on the other hand, investors overestimated the firm's information risk and assumed too high an expected return, the stock price will show a positive abnormal performance. Thus, this theory can accommodate all abnormal returns, both underperformance as well as overperformance, and is thus potentially able to explain the full cross-sectional variation in abnormal performance.

The intuition behind the information risk explanation is as follows. While cash flows are the ultimate construct for valuation, it can be a misleading picture of the economic performance for single periods as cash flows are influenced by the timing of cash receipts and cash payments. Earnings are the combination of cash flows and accrual adjustments. The latter reflect management's estimates and judgments, and are by definition affected by information uncertainty.[30] This issue is especially acute for young firms that are far from steady state, i.e., the IPO setting is one where there is scope for substantial information uncertainty. Taking earnings as a key piece of information, this study uses the perceived earnings quality as proxy for the more comprehensive notion of information quality. Thus, the metric reflects what investors perceive as good or bad quality and no model is needed to detect earnings management as in Teoh et al. (1998) or any other discretionary action.

30 Specifically, accruals are inherently subject to estimation uncertainty. In addition, the inherent uncertainty can be exacerbated or mitigated by discretionary managerial financial reporting choices, so-called discretionary accruals.

At the time of the offering, information quality is hard to estimate by investors. The evaluation of information uncertainty requires an announcement containing management's expectation about an uncertain future development and a later realization of this announcement, reflected in financial statements in general and earnings in particular. There is little incentive, but potentially large proprietary costs for non-public firms to make firm-specific information public, especially information about their profitability. In addition, pre-issue media coverage is an exception (Rao 1993). Thus, there are few, if any, information releases from which information reliability could be inferred, even if the financial statements in the prospectus contain the realized values.

One potential source to infer information about future cash flows from is the accruals adjustment in earnings. But the accruals adjustment in earnings contains, among other things, management's expectation of future cash flows (which are by definition uncertain). The accuracy of present accruals mapping into subsequent cash flows is, of all earnings quality metrics in the literature, best captured by accruals quality (AQ) as developed by Dechow and Dichev (2002). This metric is – as outlined in Chapter 3 – used to form an accruals quality mimicking factor for an asset pricing regression. The factor loadings (e-loadings) themselves are a valid construct capturing information quality: The higher the e-loading, the poorer the information quality. Although the e-loading has far less stringent data requirements than the AQ measure, a time-series of returns is still needed. By definition, this data is not available for newly public firms. An expectation about the firm's information risk must be imputed in the expected returns of IPO firms by rational investors. I proxy for this expected value with the average e-loading of the same industry in the prior (calendar) year.

The rationale for the valuation relying on an industry average is founded on prior literature. Ritter (1998) emphasizes that the valuation of an IPO is, in general, not different from the valuation of any other stock. Because of the difficulties of predicting future cash flows for young growth companies, however, he recommends using price multiples from comparable firms with similar characteristics instead of a discounted cash flow model. For the general firm, Alford (1992) provides evidence for comparable firms being best taken from the same industry. Specifically, he shows that forecasting errors are minimal when the forecast is based on an industry average price multiple such as the price-earnings ratio. Kim and Ritter (1999) confirm the validity of valuing IPO stocks using industry price multiples and firm-specific earnings forecasts. In summary, both normative texts and descriptive research indicate that the industry is able to deliver valid proxies for valuations.[31]

31 Note that the lagged average industry e-loading might not be investors' true expected value. I

In the post-issue period, the firm publicly disseminates information via various channels. Investors are able to compare realizations to earlier announcement and to verify information. This gradual procedure leads to an estimate of the firm-specific information quality and offers the possibility of replacing the initial expectation with the firm-specific information risk. Assuming rational expectations, the expected value for information risk and the realized information risk should be the same on average. In other words, the mean/median deviation of realization from expectation should not be systematically different from zero. Furthermore, an investment in IPO firms should also offer the chance to generate abnormal profits. I hypothesize that the deviation between expected and realized information risk is directly related to long-run abnormal returns of IPO firms. If the realized information risk is higher (smaller) than the expected information risk, the stock price has to be corrected downward (upward) as the required rate of return is, ceteris paribus, higher (lower), leading to a negative (positive) abnormal return during the adjustment process. Firms with initially underestimated information risk should underperform the benchmark, firms with initially overestimated information risk should outperform. This hypothesized relation ensures that the net present value of an IPO investment could be positive (as well as negative) and still allows for heterogeneous expectations about the true value.

---

consider it likely that the expected value for information risk is a weighted average reflecting many signals about the firm's information risk. The crudeness of the industry e-loading as expected value lowers the power of my tests. One of the potential additional signals could be the seller of the stock. Brav and Gompers (1997) examine the role of venture capitalists in IPO firms and their influence on post-issue performance. Among other functions, venture capitalists provide management expertise and put management structures in place. Additionally they put their reputation at stake. Similar to the underwriting investment bank, they repeatedly bring new firms to the market and should thus be cautious not to have underperformers on their record. Both functions could, ceteris paribus, lead to higher information reliability for venture-capital-backed IPOs. The influence of managerial expertise on long-term returns for IPO firms is in the focus of Chemmanur and Paeglis (2005). In their view, better management is able to "convey the intrinsic value of their firm more credibly to outsiders." The thereby reduced information asymmetry leads to a better performance in the aftermarket. This hypothesis, however, can only be supported with a test on 3-year BHARs. When a calendar-time approach is used, the intercepts themselves and their difference between high and low management quality firms are statistically indistinguishable from zero. This could be due to the low sample size (82 to 83 months), but also to the low power of the approach to capture a priced risk. While management quality potentially has an impact on information quality, I do not limit information quality to a single factor. To the extent that management quality is only one factor and information quality, as perceived by investors, is the driving force behind abnormal IPO returns, Chemmanur and Paeglis' design simply uses too crude a proxy for information quality. In addition, there is a confounding factor: Both the venture capitalist as seller and the underwriting investment bank (whose provision depends on the offering proceeds) have an interest in a high offering price. This is also true for a management with the best intentions who faces the trade-off between spreading a more favorable or a more precise piece of information. Supported by, e.g., DuCharme, Malatesta, and Sefcik (2004) and Teoh et al. (1998), management tends to present more favorable information.

Both Francis et al. (2004b) and this study link financial anomalies to information risk and are consistent with a broad efficient market definition that incorporates imperfect information credibility. However, the approaches differ in an important aspect. Whereas Francis et al. assume perfect knowledge of information risk, my study starts from the premise that firm-specific information risk is unknown and has to be estimated. As such, it is the uncertainty about the true firm-specific information risk and not the uncertainty about the quality of new information that has to be resolved in my setting of IPO firms. Not information risk itself, but the deviation of realized from expected information risk serves as the explanatory variable for the abnormal returns.

5. Tests with Abnormal Portfolio Returns

5.1 Construction of the IPO sample

Initial public offerings from 1980 to 2002 are from the Securities Data Company (SDC) database. Similar to Chemmanur and Paeglis (2005) and Lowry and Schwert (2004), real estate investment trusts (REITs) (SIC 6798) and closed-end funds (SIC 6726) are dropped from the sample. Following Ritter (1991) and Teoh et al. (1998), I also exclude so-called penny stocks with an offer price of one dollar or less and unit offerings from my sample.[32]

Monthly prices and returns as well as the number of shares outstanding from January 1980 to December 2003 are obtained from the Center for Research in Security Prices (CRSP). The price and number of shares outstanding are only used to calculate beginning-of-month market capitalization figures which in turn serve as weights in the value-weighted tests. IPOs are required to have data on CRSP as listed at one of the three major stock exchanges in the U.S. (NYSE, AMEX or NASDAQ) within two calendar months after the offering month. Similar to Ritter (1991), the stock return from the day to the end of the initial listing month is not considered; the returns series for the test starts in (calendar) Month 1 after the listing. When firms delist during the test periods, delisting returns are included as available on CRSP. Within the abnormal returns estimation period, further equity issuances by the same firm might occur. If this is the case, the months of, and all months following, a first seasoned equity offering (SEO) are not part of the returns series. As prior literature has also documented the abnormal performance subsequent to SEOs (see, e.g., Mitchell and Stafford 2000), the inclusion of these events could potentially overstate the magnitude and especially the persistence of the post-IPO abnormal returns. Returns are winsorized at the one-percent level on an annual basis (results are not sensitive to this winsorization).

Daily returns, also obtained from CRSP, are used to calculate e-loadings for IPO firms. Like in the monthly returns sample, daily returns in the first month and the month of a seasoned equity offering are excluded. I require at least 100 trading days between Month 1 and 12 after the offering to calculate the event-time e-loadings.[33] The

---

32 Units consist of an equity share and a warrant. As only the equity part is publicly traded, the return for investors cannot be calculated.

33 If an SEO occurs within this first year, all daily returns of and after the SEO month are excluded

difference from the method as presented in Chapter 3 is the measurement in event time rather than calendar time. Further, I limit the analysis to e-loadings from firm-specific 4-factor regressions:[34]

$$R_{j,t} - R_{F,t} = \alpha_j + \beta_j(R_{M,t} - R_{F,t}) + s_j SMB_t + h_j HML_t + e_j AQfactor_t + \epsilon_{j,t} \quad (7)$$

In this event-time measurement, t are all trading days in the first year after the IPO with returns data and e_j is the e-loading for IPO firm j. Because of the minimal data requirement, the e-loading as information risk metric for an IPO firm is attainable much earlier than other earnings quality measures. E-loadings data for all firms with 100 trading days in a given year is used to calculate annual industry averages. They are lagged by one year such that the average e-loading serves as expected value for all IPOs in the respective industry in the following calendar year. The deviation variable is the firm-specific e-loading e_j as measured over the first event year (realization) less the mean industry e-loading, lagged by one year, $\overline{e_{Ind.}}$, as proxy for the expected value of information risk.

$$Dev_j = e_j - \overline{e_{Ind.}} \quad (8)$$

The sample selection procedure yields a final sample of 6,138 IPO firms. The year distribution in Table 3, Panel A, shows the general increase in offerings until the mid-90s with a maximum of 643 firms in 1996. There are fewer issues in the early and late years of the sample period. Panel B is consistent with prior evidence in that the sample is clustered by industry. Almost 18% of the sample is in the computers industry, followed by electronic equipment and restaurants with 429 and 396 issues, respectively. The tobacco and generally the natural resources industries listed a small number of new firms.

---

from the estimation.

34 E-loadings from augmented CAPM regressions yield the same result.

Table 3: Distribution of IPO Sample by Year and Industry

The 48-industry classification in Panel B is taken from Fama and French (1997).

Panel A: Firm distribution by year

Year	# IPOs	Year	# IPOs
1980	58		
1981	179	1992	359
1982	71	1993	486
1983	380	1994	401
1984	174	1995	397
1985	178	1996	643
1986	371	1997	447
1987	290	1998	267
1988	122	1999	371
1989	124	2000	318
1990	102	2001	77
1991	248	2002	75
		Total	6,138

Panel B: Firm distribution by industry

Industry Name	Ind. Code	# IPOs
Agriculture	1	25
Food Products	2	70
Candy & Soda	3	9
Beer & Liquor	4	19
Tobacco Products	5	5
Recreation	6	71
Entertainment	7	124
Printing and Publishing	8	32
Consumer Goods	9	91
Apparel	10	75
Healthcare	11	155
Medical Equipment	12	252
Pharmaceutical Products	13	306
Chemicals	14	49
Rubber and Plastic Products	15	48
Textiles	16	34
Construction Materials	17	63

Table 3 Panel B (continued)

Industry Name	Ind. Code	# IPOs
Construction	18	71
Steel Works Etc	19	57
Fabricated Products	20	15
Machinery	21	156
Electrical Equipment	22	60
Automobiles and Trucks	23	44
Aircraft	24	62
Shipbuilding, Railroad Equipment	25	11
Defense	26	10
Precious Metals	27	7
Non-Metallic and Industrial Metal Mines	28	10
Coal	29	9
Petroleum and Natural Gas	30	7
Utilities	31	127
Communication	32	87
Personal Services	33	238
Business Services	34	85
Computers	35	1,079
Electronic Equipment	36	429
Measuring and Control Equipment	37	378
Business Supplies	38	143
Shipping Containers	39	39
Transportation	40	20
Wholesale	41	151
Retail	42	235
Restaurants, Hotels, Motels	43	396
Banking	44	144
Insurance	45	295
Real Estate	46	199
Trading	47	29
Other	48	117
	Total	6,138

5.2 Calendar-time portfolios from the full IPO sample

The monthly returns of the IPO firms are used to form calendar-time portfolios for the test of long-term abnormal returns. Requiring a certain number of firms for a given month-portfolio represents a trade-off between the idiosyncratic risk argument by Loughran and Ritter (2000) and the continuity of the resulting time series of returns. On the one hand, a larger number of firms in the portfolio decreases the likelihood of a few firms dominating the results. As Loughran and Ritter point out, having more firms generally leads to lower standard errors and higher testing power, in particular for value-weighted portfolios. On the other hand, a more stringent requirement on the number of firms leads to a larger drop in calendar-month observations and thus reduces the power of abnormal returns tests. Mitchell and Stafford (2000) add that a certain number of firms have to be required to control for some of the heteroscedasticity effects in the time series. For their sample, they simulate that their requirement of 10 firms each month serves this purpose. In this work, portfolios from the full sample of firms have to fulfill the requirement of 12 firms per month with returns data. In my main tests, I split the sample of firms into quartiles. To arrive at a consistent time-series and make results to the full-sample results, I require 3 firms per month to form a quartile portfolio. While this number might seem low with regard to the 10 firms in Mitchell and Stafford (2000), I include an additional control for heteroscedasticity using the GARCH (1,1) technique.[35]

The IPOs in my sample take place from January 1980 to December 2002; the period over which abnormal returns are estimated theoretically ranges from January 1980 to December 2003 (288 months). The actual length of the time series of portfolio returns, however, depends on the portfolio inclusion rule.[36] As only 11 earlier IPOs have returns data for June 1980, the first portfolio meeting the requirement of 12 firms can be constructed in July 1980. I form different portfolios containing firms in their months 1 to 12 (1 to 24, 1 to 36) after the event, labeled '1 Year' ('2 Years', '3 Years') in the following tables. For example, a firm with an IPO in January 1980 is included in the '1 Year' ('2 Years', '3 Years') calendar-time portfolios from February 1980 to January 1981 (1982, 1983). Naturally, the first seven time-series observations from July 1980 to January 1981 are equal across the three portfolio inclusion rules. The last '1 Year'

---

35 In a sensitivity test, I require 10 firms per quartile portfolio. This more stringent requirement only slightly cuts down the number of monthly observations (271 returns for the '1 Year' portfolios; 278 for the '2 Years' and '3 Years' portfolios). Results are unaffected.

36 The design of the main tests assures that there are no months missing in the time series.

portfolio is for November 2003, as only 4 firms in the sample went public in December 2002. Thus, the time-series of '1 Year' portfolio returns has 281 observations. The time series of portfolios with inclusion rules allowing for older firms, '2 Years' and '3 Years', include an observation for December 2003 and therefore consist of 282 observations. For each portfolio inclusion rule, Table 4 provides descriptive statistics on equal-weighted and value-weighted portfolios' excess returns and the number of firms included. The last row of each panel contains the average market capitalization of the firms in the portfolios. Panel A describes the time series when only one-year-old firms are included into the portfolios. Panels B and C provide the same data items for portfolios with two- and three-year-old firms.

The distribution of excess returns (not the abnormal returns to be analyzed below) reveals skewness to the left. Negative outliers in portfolio returns of all panels yield to a mean much lower than the distribution median. This is partially due to October 1987, August 1998 and November 2000.[37] Across all panels, value-weighted portfolios earn more than equal-weighted portfolios. Whereas the median (mean) return for value-weighted portfolios ranges from 1.27% to 1.44% (0.59% to 0.83%), the median (mean) equal-weighted return is 1.00% to 1.04% (0.22% to 0.48%). Firms of age 1 - 12 months are a subset of the firms of 1 - 24 months and those, in turn, are a subset of the group of firms that are at most three years old. By definition, the number of firms in the portfolio is increasing over the panels. The average number of firms in individual monthly portfolios is relatively high; only 10% of the '1 Year' portfolios consists of less than 74 firms. The average portfolio size is 250, the mean size of the '3 Years' portfolios is 608 firms. The standard deviation of the returns series is therefore expected and found to be high in Panel A, although the difference across panels is relatively small. The varying number of firms in the portfolio also emphasizes the need for heteroscedasticity-controlling techniques in the abnormal returns analyses. As pointed out earlier, however, this is less of an issue in the tests on the full sample where at least 12 firms per monthly portfolio are required.

The monthly excess returns of equal- and value-weighted portfolios, $R^{EW}_{p,m} - R_{F,m}$ and $R^{VW}_{p,m} - R_{F,m}$, respectively, serve as dependent variables in the asset pricing regressions. As outlined in Chapter 4, I use ordinary-least-squares regressions as my main design for comparability reasons, but also test my hypotheses with the GARCH (1,1) model that allows for a time-varying error variance.

[37] Note that this extreme observation only occurs in the distribution of excess returns; in contrast, abnormal returns measurement accounts for the general market movements.

Table 4: Descriptive Statistics on Calendar-Time Portfolios

The time series of monthly excess returns of value- and equal-weighted calendar-time portfolios are labeled 'Exc. Return (VW)' and 'Exc. Return (EW)', respectively. Statistics on the number of firms in the portfolios are given in the last line of each panel. '1 Year' ('2 Years', '3 Years') portfolios are portfolios containing firms with first returns data after issuance within the last (last two, last three) year(s). The mean market capitalization is the portfolio's market capitalization over the number of firms included in the portfolio.

Panel A: '1 Year' Portfolios (281 months)

	Mean	Std. Dev.	10%ile	25%ile	Median	75%ile	90%ile
Exc. Return (VW)	0.83%	8.31%	-8.15%	-4.15%	1.32%	5.75%	9.77%
Exc. Return (EW)	0.36%	8.45%	-9.17%	-4.27%	1.04%	5.52%	10.03%
# Firms	250	149	74	120	237	367	450
Mean Mkt. Cap.	304.33	358.54	56.00	100.47	159.77	283.85	845.35

Panel B: '2 Years' Portfolios (282 months)

	Mean	Std. Dev.	10%ile	25%ile	Median	75%ile	90%ile
Exc. Return (VW)	0.59%	7.90%	-8.32%	-3.98%	1.27%	5.40%	9.48%
Exc. Return (EW)	0.22%	8.34%	-9.05%	-4.60%	1.01%	4.75%	10.12%
# Firms	451	237	161	228	468	610	776
Mean Mkt. Cap.	288.58	325.39	57.14	91.98	165.07	297.56	759.17

Panel C: '3 Years' Portfolios (282 months)

	Mean	Std. Dev.	10%ile	25%ile	Median	75%ile	90%ile
Exc. Return (VW)	0.68%	7.57%	-7.96%	-3.76%	1.44%	5.43%	9.07%
Exc. Return (EW)	0.48%	8.18%	-8.78%	-4.82%	1.00%	4.86%	9.97%
# Firms	608	297	234	375	578	832	1048
Mean Mkt. Cap.	257.92	255.17	57.27	85.89	165.00	311.80	596.89

OLS:

$$R^w_{p,m} - R_{F,m} = \alpha^w_p + \beta^w_p(R_{M,m} - R_{F,m}) + s^w_p SMB_m + h^w_p HML_m + \epsilon^w_{p,m} \tag{9}$$

GARCH:

$$R^w_{p,m} - R_{F,m} = \alpha^w_p + \beta^w_p(R_{M,m} - R_{F,m}) + s^w_p SMB_m + h^w_p HML_m + \epsilon^w_{p,m} \tag{10a}$$

$$\sigma^2(\epsilon^w_{p,m}) = \gamma_0 + \gamma_1\sigma^2_{\epsilon,m-1} + \gamma_2\epsilon^2_{m-1} + \gamma_3 n_m \tag{10b}$$

The superscript w stands for either equal- or value-weighted. $R_{M,m}$ is the value-weighted CRSP market index, $R_{F,m}$ the risk-free rate in (calendar) month m. SMB_m is the monthly return on the zero-investment portfolio which is long in small firms and short in big firms ('small minus big'); HML_m is the monthly return on the zero-investment portfolio which is long in high-BM firms and short in low-BM firms ('high minus low'). The construction of the zero-investment portfolios controls for the respective other factor, such that small and big firms are of similar average BM, while high-BM and low-BM are of similar size.[38] $\sigma^2(\epsilon^w_{p,m})$ is the variance of the error term $\epsilon^w_{p,m}$, modeled as a function of its lagged value (autoregressive component), the squared lagged error term and the number of firms in the portfolio, n_m. In both specifications, the regression intercept α^w_p is interpreted as the monthly abnormal return, i.e., the return unexplained by the asset pricing model.

Table 5 presents the intercepts for value-weighted (Panel A) and equal-weighted calendar-time portfolios (Panel B). Because some authors use investment horizons[39] longer than three years after the initial offering, I extend the number of portfolio inclusion rules for the initial set of tables and show the abnormal returns on holding IPO stocks for up to 6 years after the initial offering. As outlined above, the number of observations cannot exceed 282 months, ranging from July 1980 to December 2003. For the portfolio strategy that holds only stocks within their first year, the length of the time series is 281 months; December 2003 is missing because of too few firms in the portfolio for that month.

In Panel A, the abnormal return estimates for value-weighted portfolios range from -0.11% to 0.28% per month. While one might argue about their actual economic significance, none of the estimates is statistically significant at conventional levels. Common holding periods in long-term studies such as three years or five years yield an abnormal return of 0.05% (t = 0.34) and -0.11% (t = -0.81) per month, respectively. I conclude from these results that the 3-factor model properly describes the expected returns of value-weighted portfolios and there is no evidence of the full IPO sample exhibiting abnormal returns.

Turning to the equal-weighted portfolio results in Panel B, the obvious difference is that now each estimate is negative. But in the OLS specification, only the portfolio with firms not older than two years produces a significantly negative abnormal return

38 For details on the construction, refer to Fama and French (1993).

39 The strategy mimicked here is to hold calendar-time portfolios of IPO stocks with changing compositions over the full time series. 'Investment horizon' and 'holding period' thus denotes the length of the time period over which a specific stock is part of the portfolio.

of -0.54% (t = -2.58). Investing only in one-year-old firms yields -0.31% (t = -1.51), which is essentially the same as when extending the holding period for each firm to three years (-0.31%, $t = -1.44$). The GARCH model leads to more conservative abnormal returns only for the first three strategies and generally increases the significance over all horizons compared to the OLS test-statistics, consistent with the GARCH model being better specified. However, in general, the difference between the OLS and the GARCH results is relatively small.

The discussion of previous literature has shown that information risk is priced by investors. Therefore, information risk should arguably be included in the estimation of expected returns in order to yield an empirically well-specified model.[40] I augment the 3-factor regression by a monthly *AQfactor*. The construction is very similar to the procedure described in Chapter 3. Each month (not each day), I rank all firms according to their accruals quality, and form a zero-investment portfolio with monthly returns which is long in the top 40% and short in the bottom 40% of firms with AQ data in the respective month. At the end, I obtain a monthly *AQfactor* (denoted $AQfactor_m$), which is included in the expected returns model:

OLS:

$$\begin{aligned} R^w_{p,m} - R_{F,m} &= \alpha^w_p + \beta^w_p(R_{M,m} - R_{F,m}) + s^w_p SMB_m + h^w_p HML_m \\ &\quad + e^w_p AQfactor_m + \epsilon^w_{p,m} \end{aligned} \tag{11}$$

GARCH:

$$\begin{aligned} R^w_{p,m} - R_{F,m} =& \alpha^w_p + \beta^w_p(R_{M,m} - R_{F,m}) + s^w_p SMB_m + h^w_p HML_m \\ &+ e^w_p AQfactor_m + \epsilon^w_{p,m} \end{aligned} \tag{12a}$$

$$\sigma^2(\epsilon^w_{p,m}) = \gamma_0 + \gamma_1\sigma^2_{\epsilon,m-1} + \gamma_2\epsilon^2_{m-1} + \gamma_3 n_m \tag{12b}$$

Note that the inclusion of the information risk factor in the OLS regression is conceptually different from the calculation of firm-specific e-loadings. E-loadings are calculated with daily data in firm-specific regressions over the first year after the issuance and are held constant throughout the analyses in this work. Those e-loadings are then used to calculate the deviation variable. With this regression here, I price a calendar-time portfolio over the full sample period from 1980 to 2003 using monthly returns observations.

---

[40] Aboody et al. (2005) use a similar argument to include information risk in their setting where the information asymmetry is exploited by insider trading.

Table 5: Abnormal Returns on IPO Portfolios (3-Factor Model)

The table displays the intercepts from Fama-French asset pricing regressions on value-weighted and equal-weighted portfolio returns. The weights are adjusted at the beginning of each month according to the last closing price and the number of shares outstanding of the previous month. The first column contains the portfolio inclusion rule: Firms are included within their first year, within their first two years, after the month of their initial listing. The second column, labeled '# Obs.', contains the number of months in the time-series. The abnormal returns with the associated t-statistics for ordinary-least-squares regressions ('OLS') and 'GARCH' (1,1) simultaneous regressions are in columns 3 and 4, respectively.

Panel A: Abnormal return on value-weighted portfolios

		OLS		**GARCH**	
	# Obs.	Abnormal Return	t-stat	Abnormal Return	t-stat
1 Year	281	0.28%	1.28	0.23%	1.44
2 Years	282	-0.01%	-0.07	-0.02%	-0.12
3 Years	282	0.05%	0.34	0.02%	0.16
4 Years	282	0.00%	0.00	-0.03%	-0.25
5 Years	282	-0.11%	-0.81	-0.05%	-0.52
6 Years	282	-0.07%	-0.53	0.04%	0.36
Mean		0.02%		0.03%	
Median		-0.01%		0.00%	

Panel B: Abnormal return on equal-weighted portfolios

		OLS		**GARCH**	
	# Obs.	Abnormal Return	t-stat	Abnormal Return	t-stat
1 Year	281	-0.31%	-1.51	-0.19%	-1.42
2 Years	282	-0.54%	-2.58	-0.48%	-4.25
3 Years	282	-0.31%	-1.44	-0.25%	-1.94
4 Years	282	-0.19%	-0.92	-0.26%	-1.96
5 Years	282	-0.12%	-0.59	-0.25%	-1.88
6 Years	282	-0.11%	-0.54	-0.24%	-1.96
Mean		-0.26%		-0.28%	
Median		-0.25%		-0.25%	

Intuitively (and as shown by Ecker et al. 2006), newly listed firms on average have higher e-loadings than seasoned firms and the mean value of the *AQfactor* over the sample period is positive. Therefore, the inclusion of information risk in the asset pricing model should lead to higher expected returns and lower abnormal returns. Table 6 shows that this is indeed the case. Intercepts are always smaller than or comparable to the intercepts in the 3-factor model. Value-weighted portfolios still do not show any underperformance; all intercepts are far from being statistically significant. The results on equal-weighted portfolios, however, deviate somewhat from the previous results. As in Table 5, the '2 Years' portfolio exhibits the lowest abnormal return of -0.67% per month (t = -3.79) and -0.55% (t = -4.74) in the GARCH regression. All intercepts are significantly negative up to a four-year holding period in the OLS model; the respective t-values are always below -2.00. Even when the holding period is extended to five and six years, the abnormal return is still -0.29% (t = -1.91) and -0.27% (t = -1.86) per month. Again, the GARCH model exhibits generally higher significance levels.

As in Table 5, the different results for equal- and value-weighted portfolios leave the impression that small firms might drive the underperformance of the portfolios. One possible explanation could be a bad model for the expected returns of the smallest firms in my sample. On the other hand, if the asset pricing model captures the full size effect, size would have explanatory power for underperformance. This is consistent with prior research by Mitchell and Stafford (2000), Brav et al. (2000) and Fama (1998) that underperformance is restricted to tiny firms. I investigate size issues in detail in Section 5.4.2.

5.3 Persistence tests

Concentrating on the equal-weighted portfolios for the moment, an interesting pattern emerges from the intercepts in Table 5 and Table 6. Starting from the '2 Years' portfolios, the abnormal return in the OLS specification becomes less negative with increasing portfolio horizon. This raises the question how long the abnormal return after the initial offering actually persists.

A first, and rather crude, test design for this question is to examine the IPO sample separately for each year after the issuance. The altered portfolio inclusion rule is as follows. The '1st year' portfolio includes all firms listed within the last year and is therefore the same as before. All further portfolios, however, exclude firms that are included in the same month's portfolio when a strategy with shorter investment horizon is applied. In essence, for a firm to enter the '2nd year' portfolio, it has to be listed

Table 6: Abnormal Returns on IPO Portfolios (4-Factor Model)

For a description of the table content see Table 5. The asset pricing model employed here includes the monthly *AQfactor*.

Panel A: Abnormal return on value-weighted portfolios

		OLS		GARCH	
	# Obs.	Abnormal Return	t-stat	Abnormal Return	t-stat
1 Year	281	0.26%	1.19	0.21%	1.35
2 Years	282	-0.03%	-0.19	-0.02%	-0.17
3 Years	282	0.02%	0.16	0.00%	0.04
4 Years	282	-0.02%	-0.15	-0.03%	-0.36
5 Years	282	-0.13%	-1.00	-0.07%	-0.62
6 Years	282	-0.09%	-0.72	0.03%	0.31
Mean		0.00%		0.02%	
Median		-0.03%		-0.01%	

Panel B: Abnormal return on equal-weighted portfolios

		OLS		GARCH	
	# Obs.	Abnormal Return	t-stat	Abnormal Return	t-stat
1 Year	281	-0.41%	-2.11	-0.26%	-1.89
2 Years	282	-0.67%	-3.79	-0.55%	-4.74
3 Years	282	-0.46%	-2.72	-0.41%	-2.81
4 Years	282	-0.35%	-2.22	-0.42%	-2.82
5 Years	282	-0.29%	-1.91	-0.38%	-2.48
6 Years	282	-0.27%	-1.86	-0.34%	-2.61
Mean		-0.41%		-0.39%	
Median		-0.38%		-0.40%	

between 13 and 24 months ago. Firms in the '3rd year' portfolio have to be listed between 25 and 36 months ago, etc. An example will illustrate the inclusion rule. A firm that is listed in January 1990 and has returns data starting from February 1990 will enter the '1st year' portfolio from February 1990 to January 1991, the '2nd year' portfolio from February 1991 to January 1992 and the 3rd year portfolio from February 1992 to January 1993.

There are two reasons why the number of months for such a portfolio rule declines. In general, the longer firms are listed, the higher is the likelihood of a delisting for any reason; the number of IPO firms that survived seven years and thus enter the '8th year' portfolio is by definition smaller than the number of firms that survived a shorter period. There is a second reason why the number of months must decline. The portfolio with firms in their first year can be constructed in July 1980. As the sample of IPOs starts no earlier than in 1980, the first portfolio with at least one year old firms ('2nd Year' portfolios) can only be built in July 1981.[41] With each additional year of required IPO firms' age, 12 monthly observations are by definition lost. When the loss exceeds 12 months in some of the cases, additional months are lost because of delistings.

For value-weighted portfolios (results not tabulated), intercepts are generally not significant (consistent with the value-weighted results in Table 5 and Table 6). The results for equal-weighted portfolio returns are summarized in Table 7. Both OLS and GARCH results show no significant abnormal returns from the third year on after the offering. As no qualitative differences prevail, I discuss only the OLS results. For the 3-factor model, only the intercept for the two-year-old firms' portfolio is significant ($t =$ -3.46) and with -0.96% per month low in economic terms. Turning to the 4-factor model results, the abnormal returns are generally smaller, as expected. The abnormal return on the '2nd year' portfolio is now -1.20% ($t =$ -5.42). In addition, the significance level of the '1st year' abnormal return increases. Whereas the intercepts here are for separate firm ages, the intercepts in the two preceding tables are always 'averages' as the holding periods always start in the month after the first listing. Across the panels, the intercepts are therefore increasing at a higher rate than in Table 5 or Table 6.

Note that while the abnormal returns when holding the stocks from the first month on give the impression to persist for at least four years (Table 6), the results in Panel B indicate that the persistence is limited to the first two years after the issue. There is no difference in the persistence of negative 3-factor and 4-factor model intercepts. It is only the magnitude of the 4-factor abnormal return in the second year that makes the abnormal return in Table 6 seem to persist for a longer time.

Ideally, one wants to estimate the persistence of a significant mispricing on a month-specific (and not year-specific) level. The trade-off is, however, that noise in the abnormal return estimation for the portfolio is increasing with shorter investment horizon for individual stocks. At the same time, the number of IPOs in each sample month must

41 The reader will notice the loss of only 11 firms going from the '1st year' to the '2nd year' portfolio in Table 7. This is because 'December 2003' enters the sample. More than 12 firms newly listed from December 2001 to November 2002, but only four in December 2002.

Table 7: Abnormal Returns on Equal-weighted Portfolios For Separate Firm Ages

The table displays the intercepts from 3-factor and 4-factor asset pricing regressions on equal-weighted portfolio returns. The first column contains the portfolio inclusion rule: The '1st year' portfolio is the same as the portfolio '1 Year' in Table 5. When firms listed between 13 and 24 months ago (are in their second year), they are included in the '2nd year' portfolio, and so on. The second column, labeled '# Obs.', contains the number of months in the time series. The abnormal returns with the associated t-statistics for ordinary-least-squares (OLS) regressions and 'GARCH' (1,1) simultaneous regressions are in columns 3 and 4, respectively.

Panel A: 3-factor model intercepts

		OLS		**GARCH**	
	# Obs.	Abnormal Return	t-stat	Abnormal Return	t-stat
1st Year	281	-0.31%	-1.51	-0.19%	-1.42
2nd Year	270	-0.96%	-3.46	-0.78%	-5.45
3rd Year	258	0.09%	0.30	0.14%	0.57
4th Year	243	0.16%	0.61	-0.09%	-0.45
5th Year	231	0.26%	0.94	0.32%	1.14
6th Year	219	0.20%	0.76	0.33%	1.40

Panel B: 4-factor model intercepts

		OLS		**GARCH**	
	# Obs.	Abnormal Return	t-stat	Abnormal Return	t-stat
1st Year	281	-0.41%	-2.11	-0.26%	-1.89
2nd Year	270	-1.20%	-5.42	-0.94%	-6.28
3rd Year	258	-0.19%	-0.79	-0.18%	-0.94
4th Year	243	-0.09%	-0.46	-0.16%	-0.96
5th Year	231	-0.03%	-0.16	-0.03%	-0.14
6th Year	219	-0.11%	-0.52	-0.11%	-0.49

be large enough to form a '1st month' portfolio. Therefore, I refine the methodology in two ways. First, I use rolling time windows; starting with the same portfolio as in Table 7 from Month 1 to Month 12, I continue estimating abnormal returns for the portfolio of firms in their months 2 to 13, 3 to 14, and so on. Second, I diminish the window length to six and three months, respectively. Shorter-horizon abnormal returns will revert more quickly and generally show more pronounced abnormal returns. This pattern can be expected as less weight is placed on the trailing observations for shorter windows and abnormal returns are therefore less 'diluted' by months without abnormal returns. For the reasons discussed above, the sample size reduces when firms that have been listed for a longer period are included (but not as quickly as in the previous table).[42]

Figure 1 depicts the abnormal return estimates (OLS) for the different window lengths where the numbers on the x-axis are the last month of the estimation window.[43] As expected, the portfolios for longer time windows show smoother abnormal returns series, as the estimation precision increases. Most comparable to the previous results, the series of the rolling 12-months-window shows the highest underperformance of -1.18% per month (t = -4.54) when firms have been listed between 9 and 20 months. The 6-months-window portfolio returns underperform the benchmark by -1.46% (t = -5.08) in the Months 12 to 17. By definition, the first observation attainable is the abnormal return for the portfolio of one to three months old firms. Letting the firms become increasingly older, the abnormal return of this '3 Months' portfolio rapidly decreases with the extreme value of -1.42% per month (t = -4.65) in Months 12 to 14. I assess the persistence of underperformance by taking the end month of the last estimation period before the abnormal return estimate is no longer different from zero at the 5% level for the first time after the lowest point estimate. IPO firms included in a 3-months (6-months, 12-months) portfolio do not show any underperformance after Month 18 (22, 27) (indicated by the filled dots in the graphs).[44]

As pointed out earlier, abnormal returns should be estimated controlling for information risk. When *AQfactor* is included in the asset pricing model, the pattern of the graphs in Figure 2 is seemingly similar to Figure 1. In general, the abnormal return estimate for each end month decrease. Due to this shift, the persistence of the abnormal return extends to 26 (29, 33) months after the issuance for a rolling 3- (6-, 12) months window. Importantly, from this month onwards, the abnormal returns randomly fluctuate around zero.[45]

---

42 Specifically, the decreasing number of monthly abnormal returns in the sample has only a negligible influence on the test statistics for the average abnormal returns.

43 Detailed results for the OLS asset pricing regression as presented here and additionally for the GARCH specification are tabulated in the appendix, Table A.1, in Appendix.

44 As the abnormal return does not persist longer for the full sample, I limit the analyses in the following sections to holding periods up to three years, allowing for differential persistence in subsamples.

45 I ascribe the apparent increase in the estimates variance in later event month to the smaller sample size.

Figure 1: Abnormal Portfolio Returns for Rolling Short Investment Horizons (OLS) (3-factor)

The graphs show abnormal returns for rolling 3-months, 6-months and 12-months windows that determine the firms to be included in the monthly portfolios. The labels on the x-axis are the respective end months of the time windows.

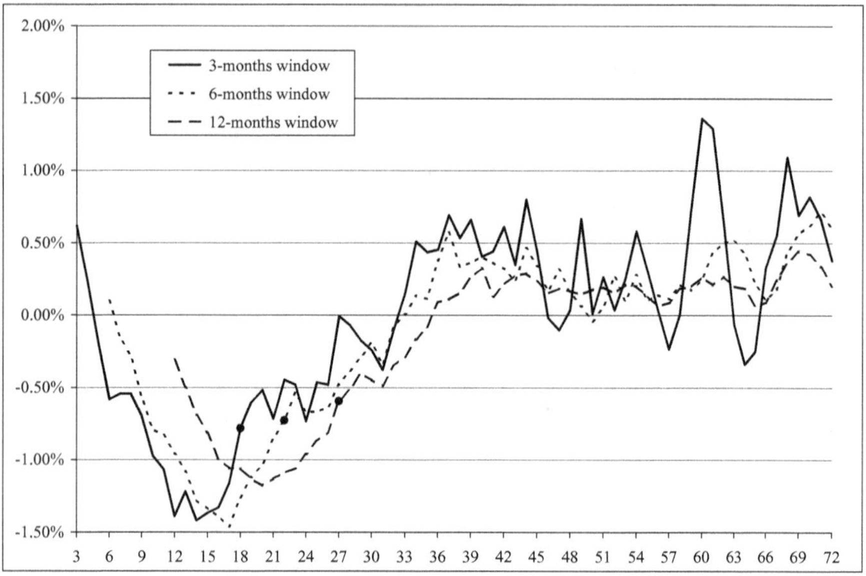

As discussed in Section 4.1.2, the use of BHARs does not allow any inferences on the persistence of abnormal returns. Furthermore, Mitchell and Stafford (2000) show that BHARs magnify the abnormal return estimate with an increase in investment horizon, even when the mispricing is concentrated in the early part of the estimation period. The empirical results above indicate that this is indeed the case. The commonly used 3-year BHAR and CAR will, on average, only contain 18 months of underperformance. In the remaining 18 months, the return of IPO stocks is well described by the market factor, size and BM; 3-factor abnormal returns are not distinguishable from zero. While the problem of an exaggerated magnitude is surely of higher importance in the case of BHARs, CARs and AARs are also biased downward when months of insignificantly negative returns are included in their calculation.

To summarize the full-sample results, there is some indication that equal-weighted portfolios of the broad sample of IPO firms underperform, consistent with prior literature. However, the magnitude and the significance of the negative abnormal return

Figure 2: Abnormal Portfolio Returns for Rolling Short Investment Horizons (OLS) (4-factor)

The graphs show abnormal returns for rolling 3-months, 6-months and 12-months windows that determine the firms to be included in the monthly portfolios. The labels on the x-axis are the respective end months of the time windows. The y-axis is the abnormal return from the 4-factor model.

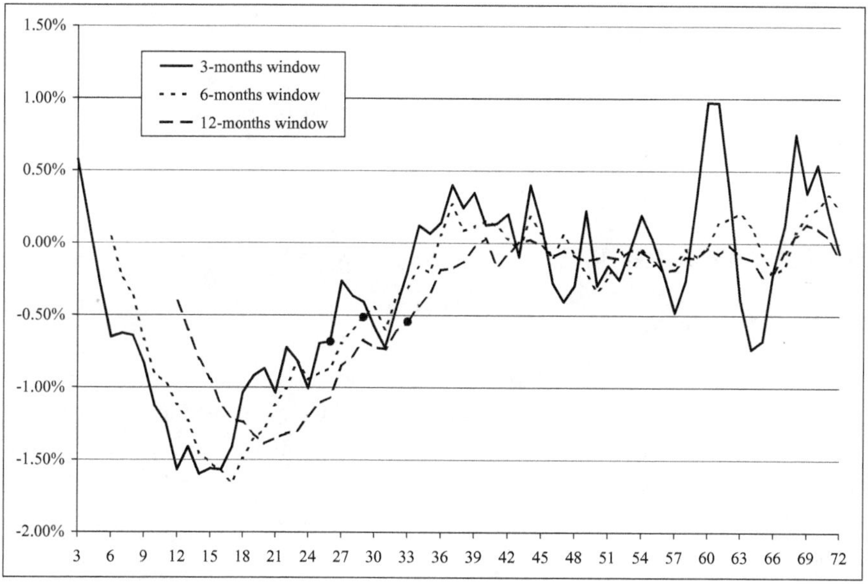

(see Table 5) are low. Both the 3-factor and the 4-factor model can explain the excess returns of value-weighted portfolios. The tests in this section show that the highest negative return occurs in the second year after the offering; the third year does not show any mispricing. When the test specification is changed to rolling time windows and the length of this window is reduced to three months, the negative 3-factor abnormal return of equal-weighted portfolios only persists until IPO firms have been listed for 18 months. It is therefore misleading to simply infer the actual persistence of an abnormal return from the horizon over which the abnormal return is measured.

Table 8: Descriptive Statistics on E-Loadings, Industry Averages and Deviation

The summarizing data is for the sample of 6,138 IPO firms. E-loadings are the coefficients on *AQfactor* in a daily 4-factor asset pricing regression over the first year of returns data. Industry Average is the lagged average of calendar-time e-loadings from all firms in the same industry. Deviation is defined as e-loading less industry average. The mean deviation is the mean e-loading less the mean industry average, the small difference is because of rounding.

	Mean	Std. Dev.	25%ile	Median	75%ile
E-loadings	0.1715	0.5389	-0.1573	0.1285	0.4656
Industry Average	0.1536	0.1131	0.0723	0.1583	0.2269
Deviation	0.0180	0.5359	-0.3006	-0.0112	0.3069

5.4 Deviation tests

5.4.1 Main results

The results for the full sample of firms set the stage for the tests of my hypothesis for abnormal performance. Only equal-weighted portfolios show a significant underperformance, value-weighted portfolio returns, for the full sample, are fully captured both by the 3-factor and 4-factor model. For this reason, and following Fama and French (1992), Fama and French (1993) who value-weight within each portfolio, I put more emphasis on value-weighted results.

I use e-loadings from all firms with the necessary data in a given calendar year in the period between 1979 and 2001. Based on the Fama and French (1997) industry classification scheme, I form 48 year-specific industry averages. The industry average is my proxy for the expected value of the information risk for an IPO in this industry in the following calendar year. The firm-specific e-loadings are calculated as outlined in Section 5.1. The realized firm-specific e-loadings less the expected value for information risk is the deviation variable from Equation (8). Descriptive data on the respective distributions of e-loadings, the industry averages and deviation for the full IPO sample are summarized in Table 8.

My hypothesis builds on Bayesian theory (e.g., DeGroot 1970). Investors form a prior belief about the information risk of a given IPO and start updating this expected value at the time of the offering. I do not make any detailed assumption concerning this gradual process. Specifically, while I use the first year of daily returns data for the estimation of firm-specific e-loadings, the time investors really need for this assessment might well differ from this year (see results on the persistence tests); it might even be firm-specific. The updating might take less time, so that no weight is placed on the initial expectation after a year. On the other hand, the gradual process might also be such that there remains a positive weight on the prior, i.e., the industry average. In the case of a still running process, my definition of deviation would understate the true difference between realized and expected value.

The deviation variable has a positive mean of 0.0180 and a negative median of -0.0112. While the mean is significantly positive at the 0.01 level, the median is not significant (p-value 0.8942). Both mean and median are close to zero in economic terms, and I interpret this as indicative that investors make little or no systematic error in the initial estimation of information risk for the full sample of IPO firms. This result is consistent with rational expectations regarding information uncertainty, where the average expectation equals the average realization.

Each month, I rank all firms (that match the portfolio inclusion rule) according to their deviation variable and form four portfolios for the lowest-, the two intermediate- and the highest-deviation firms. The initial requirement of at least 12 firms per month is thus reduced to 3.[46] This enables me to create value- and equal-weighted calendar-time portfolios for the same months as in the previous section, thus ensuring the comparability of the results.

Table 9 provides an initial analysis of the eight time series when firms are included in the first two years after the issuance (282 monthly observations). The average portfolio size is 113 firms. For each deviation quartile of firms, I report the equal- and value-weighted excess portfolio return and the mean market capitalization. As the monthly ranking procedure does not assure that the deviation is always negative for the lowest-deviation portfolio and always positive for the highest-deviation portfolio, I include descriptive data for the mean deviation per portfolio as well. The summary statistics show that the large majority (always more than 90%) of the Quartile 1 and 2 portfolios has a negative mean deviation and equivalently, the majority of the other two portfolios has a mean positive deviation. This simplifies the interpretation of the results as the average information risk for the two low-quartile portfolios has been overestimated and the information risk of the other two portfolios has been underestimated.

Independent of the weighting scheme, the mean and median excess portfolio returns are positive for the first three quartiles and negative for the last quartile, but only

[46] As noted in Footnote 4 in Chapter 5, changing this requirement to 10 firms per quartile portfolio does not affect results.

Table 9: Description of The Deviation-Quartile Calendar-Time Portfolios

The table displays descriptive data on the deviation variable and the time series of equal- and value-weighted excess portfolio returns for separate deviation quartiles. 'Size' is the mean market capitalization of the firms in the portfolios.

	Mean	Std. Dev.	10%ile	25%ile	Median	75%ile	90%ile
Quartile 1							
– Lowest Deviation							
Deviation	-0.5852	0.1083	-0.7160	-0.6560	-0.5997	-0.5159	-0.4315
Exc. Return (EW)	0.80%	7.73%	-8.33%	-4.03%	1.29%	5.57%	10.97%
Exc. Return (VW)	1.41%	8.32%	-7.74%	-3.63%	1.51%	6.13%	10.55%
Size	332.5	468.8	48.2	78.6	159.0	262.1	940.1
Quartile 2							
Deviation	-0.1321	0.0757	-0.2131	-0.1863	-0.1496	-0.0968	-0.0584
Exc. Return (EW)	0.28%	7.47%	-8.73%	-4.21%	1.12%	4.67%	8.75%
Exc. Return (VW)	0.72%	8.08%	-8.53%	-4.09%	1.26%	5.05%	9.56%
Size	325.2	343.1	59.0	91.6	189.6	382.6	906.7
Quartile 3							
Deviation	0.1580	0.1038	0.0541	0.0889	0.1227	0.1976	0.3186
Exc. Return (EW)	0.10%	8.83%	-9.36%	-4.78%	0.56%	4.73%	9.77%
Exc. Return (VW)	0.29%	8.35%	-7.98%	-3.87%	0.54%	4.78%	10.16%
Size	329.9	387.9	66.3	93.6	230.7	323.8	796.2
Quartile 4							
– Highest Deviation							
Deviation	0.7014	0.1424	0.5080	0.6129	0.6646	0.8164	0.9225
Exc. Return (EW)	-0.29%	10.69%	-11.83%	-6.27%	-0.15%	5.18%	11.54%
Exc. Return (VW)	-0.44%	11.00%	-12.58%	-6.34%	-0.19%	6.22%	11.36%
Size	166.3	193.0	39.2	56.3	91.7	153.4	407.7

the value-weighted return in the first quartile is (highly) significant. From mean and median of the excess returns only, there is also no clear domination of a weighting scheme. However, there is a clear trend across the quartiles. Equal-weighted returns monotonically decrease from 0.80% to 0.29% per month over the deviation quartiles, value-weighted returns drop from 1.41% to 0.44%. Thus, separating the sample by deviation also reveals differences in the excess returns of the portfolios.[47] Although this pattern is suggestive, it is still an open question whether the quartiles show similar *abnormal* returns patterns. As the ranking on the basis of deviation does not control

[47] As the mean risk-free rate is the same for all quartile portfolios, this is also true for raw returns.

for any risk factors, the differences in excess returns could merely reflect different risk sensitivities and thus differences in expected returns.

Similar to the full sample, the distribution of excess returns is skewed to the left in each deviation quartile. The table documents that the standard deviation of value-weighted returns is generally higher than that of equal-weighted returns with one exception (Quartile 3). This is consistent with Loughran and Ritter (2000) argument that value-weighting lowers the power of calendar-time tests, because idiosyncratic risk may not be diversified away when only a few big firms dominate the portfolios. Note that the average size of the firms in the portfolios does not show a monotonic pattern across quartiles. The mean of this distribution is almost the same for the first three quartiles, but smaller for the highest-deviation quartile. The median shows an increase over the first three deviation quartiles and a drop for the last. Obviously, small firms are overrepresented in the highest-deviation quartile. I explore this and other size-related issues in Section 5.4.2.

To estimate the abnormal returns, each time series of excess returns serves as dependent variable in the asset pricing regressions. Additionally, I form a fifth time series as the returns difference between the highest- and the lowest-deviation quartile. Note that this is not meant to be an implementable trading strategy, merely a convenient way of assessing the magnitude and the significance of the difference between the extreme quartiles. Table 10 summarizes the findings for holding periods of one to three years.

Panel A shows the intercepts when the 3-factor model serves as benchmark. The abnormal returns for the lowest-deviation quartile is 1.22% ($t = 3.91$) for a holding period of one year and, almost symmetrically, -1.27% ($t =$ -3.24) for the highest-deviation quartile. When only held for the first year, firms with the second lowest deviation also show a significant positive abnormal return of 0.63% per month ($t = 2.07$). But generally, the intermediate deviation categories do not show any abnormal performance over the different holding periods. With an increase in holding period, there is a clear trend in the extreme quartiles towards lower (absolute) abnormal performance. Lowest-deviation firms that are included for two and three years outperform the 3-factor model only by 0.88% and 0.69%, respectively. Conversely, highest-deviation firms underperform in their first two and three years by -1.09% and -0.64%. The difference between lowest and highest quartile is economically and statistically significant and decreases from -2.49% ($t =$ -4.91) to -1.34% ($t =$ -3.44) per month over the three investment horizons considered.

When the asset pricing model is augmented by *AQfactor* (Panel B), the intercepts measure abnormal returns controlling for information risk. There is still the monotonic

Table 10: Abnormal Return for Value-Weighted Deviation Quartile Portfolios

The table displays intercepts from 3-factor and 4-factor asset pricing regressions (OLS) on value-weighted excess calendar-time portfolio returns and a return on a portfolio that is long in the lowest-deviation firms and short in the highest-deviation firms. The GARCH specification leads to very similar conclusions. The results for value- and equal-weighted portfolio returns are provided in the appendix, Tables A.3 and A.4, respectively.

Panel A: 3-Factor Abnormal Returns

	1 Year (281 months)		2 Years (282 months)		3 Years (282 months)	
Deviation Quartile	Abnormal Return	t-stat	Abnormal Return	t-stat	Abnormal Return	t-stat
Lowest	1.22%	3.91	0.88%	3.72	0.69%	3.35
Q2	0.63%	2.07	0.09%	0.37	0.08%	0.44
Q3	0.05%	0.15	-0.29%	-1.10	-0.07%	-0.26
Highest	-1.27%	-3.24	-1.09%	-3.01	-0.64%	-1.99
High - Low	-2.49%	-4.91	-1.97%	-4.54	-1.34%	-3.44

Panel B: 4-Factor Abnormal Returns

	1 Year (281 months)		2 Years (282 months)		3 Years (282 months)	
Deviation Quartile	Abnormal Return	t-stat	Abnormal Return	t-stat	Abnormal Return	t-stat
Lowest	1.30%	4.23	0.93%	3.98	0.72%	3.48
Q2	0.64%	2.10	0.08%	0.35	0.08%	0.45
Q3	-0.04%	-0.11	-0.35%	-1.37	-0.13%	-0.52
Highest	-1.47%	-3.99	-1.24%	-3.65	-0.79%	-2.66
High - Low	-2.77%	-5.94	-2.17%	-5.41	-1.51%	-4.20

decrease in abnormal returns across the quartiles and also with the increase in holding period. The estimates for the intermediate quartiles change only marginally. The difference between the extreme quartiles, however, is more pronounced and more significant. The lowest quartile abnormal return is with 1.30% slightly higher as compared to the 3-factor abnormal return and the highest quartile portfolio underperforms by -1.47% per month. Overall, these results indicate that the inclusion of the information risk factor lowers the expected return for the lowest quartile and increases the expected return for the highest quartile. However, the differences are modest in economic terms.

Recall that value-weighted portfolios for the full IPO sample did not show any significant abnormal performance, regardless of the asset pricing model against which they were evaluated. Thus, the non-existence of abnormal performance for the full sample masks the fact that there is indeed an outperforming and an underperforming segment of the IPO population, with the segments partitionable on the deviation variable.

Table 11 shows the results of the deviation analysis for equal-weighted portfolios. Again, the difference between highest- and lowest-deviation quartiles declines with rising investment horizon, but the magnitude and the mean point of this difference have changed. Using the 3-factor model, the difference is -1.67% (-1.07%, -0.84%) for a holding period of one (two, three) year(s), but still highly significant. The 4-factor model again delivers more pronounced differences. Switching from value- to equal-weighted portfolios, the center of the difference between the highest and the lowest quartile has also moved, as expected from the full sample results. The average abnormal return for the full sample is -0.54% for the 3-factor and -0.67% for the 4-factor model. Both figures fall between the abnormal return estimates for the respective intermediate deviation quartiles which now show generally significant underperformance as well.

Although I report both equal- and value-weighted results, more weight should be put on the value-weighted results to answer the question of economy-wide effects (as argued by Fama 1998 and Brav et al. 2000). The results fulfill the second criterion for rational investor behavior: Investors in IPO firms do have the chance to earn positive abnormal returns as well as bear the risk of earning negative abnormal returns. Repeated investment in IPO firms therefore is not a negative NPV strategy.

The findings for both asset pricing regressions and weighting schemes provide strong support for the main hypothesis of this work. An initial underestimation of the firm's information risk (and therefore of the required rate of return) leads to a gradual downward correction of the price in the aftermarket. Conversely, if market participants initially overestimated the firm's information risk, the price has to be corrected upward as the (perceived) expected return decreases over time.

To provide more detail about the deviation portfolios, Table 12 shows the factor loadings for the regression on equal-weighted portfolio returns which holds IPO firms for two years. As expected for IPO firms, the coefficient on the market factor, beta, is greater than 1.00 for all quartiles and does not show any systematic pattern. The s-coefficient in the 3-factor regression is strictly increasing, again pointing towards the

Table 11: Abnormal Return for Equal-Weighted Deviation Quartile Portfolios

The table displays intercepts from 3-factor and 4-factor asset pricing regressions (OLS) on equal-weighted excess calendar-time portfolio returns and a return on a portfolio that is long in the lowest-deviation firms and short in the highest-deviation firms.

Panel A: 3-Factor Abnormal Returns

	1 Year (281 months)		2 Years (282 months)		3 Years (282 months)	
Deviation Quartile	Abnormal Return	t-stat	Abnormal Return	t-stat	Abnormal Return	t-stat
Lowest	0.50%	1.96	0.05%	0.26	0.24%	1.18
Q2	-0.01%	-0.02	-0.51%	-2.53	-0.40%	-2.15
Q3	-0.55%	-2.11	-0.65%	-2.58	-0.45%	-1.91
Highest	-1.17%	-2.95	-1.02%	-2.80	-0.60%	-1.63
High - Low	-1.67%	-3.59	-1.07%	-3.05	-0.84%	-2.60

Panel B: 4-Factor Abnormal Returns

	1 Year (281 months)		2 Years (282 months)		3 Years (282 months)	
Deviation Quartile	Abnormal Return	t-stat	Abnormal Return	t-stat	Abnormal Return	t-stat
Lowest	0.58%	2.33	0.03%	0.14	0.17%	0.88
Q2	-0.03%	-0.16	-0.59%	-3.06	-0.50%	-2.93
Q3	-0.70%	-2.96	-0.81%	-3.73	-0.63%	-3.29
Highest	-1.46%	-4.40	-1.30%	-4.55	-0.89%	-3.11
High - Low	-2.04%	-5.45	-1.33%	-4.70	-1.06%	-3.98

presence of a size effect, to be discussed in the following section. Much less pronounced, the h-loading is decreasing across the quartiles.

In the 4-factor model, the e-loading on the monthly *AQfactor* is increasing with deviation.[48] Apparently, the *AQfactor* takes away power from the *SMB* and *HML*

48 This is not comparable to the firm- and year-specific e-loading that is generally used in the paper. Here, it is the e-loading for the calendar-time portfolio and this loading is constant over the whole sample period from 1980 to 2003.

factors. Two of the four coefficients on *HML* are insignificant; the pattern in *SMB* loadings even reverts. Further note that the inclusion of *AQfactor* always increases the explanatory power of the regressions substantially, as indicated by the increased Adjusted R^2s. The highest incremental contribution is in the highest-deviation quartile (68.29% for the 3-factor vs. 81.51% for the 4-factor model). The significant loadings on *AQfactor* and the uniformly higher Adjusted R^2 for the 4-factor regressions compared to the 3-factor regressions prove that the systematic component of information risk in this sample is not captured by the 3-factor model. As shown above, however, inferences regarding the intercepts are relatively similar.

Table 12: Factor Loadings from Regressions on Equal-weighted Portfolio Returns

This table summarizes the coefficients and Adjusted R^2 from the regressions in Table 11, but for portfolios with two-year holding periods only (282 months-observations from July 1980 to December 2003).

Portfolio		Factor Loadings				Adj. R^2
		β (Excess Market)	s (SMB)	h (HML)	e (AQfactor)	
Lowest Deviation	Coeff.	1.2046	0.8326	-0.3140	-	75.65%
	t-stat	*18.70*	*10.26*	*-3.29*		
Q2	Coeff.	1.0434	0.9360	-0.3116	-	79.07%
	t-stat	*19.01*	*13.53*	*-3.83*		
Q3	Coeff.	1.0757	1.0387	-0.5374	-	77.32%
	t-stat	*16.44*	*12.60*	*-5.54*		
Highest Deviation	Coeff.	1.2597	1.3377	-0.6571	-	68.29%
	t-stat	*12.61*	*10.63*	*-4.43*		
Lowest Deviation	Coeff.	1.1891	0.7532	-0.2353	0.05826	84.80%
	t-stat	*24.96*	*9.79*	*-3.28*	*1.58*	
Q2	Coeff.	1.0901	0.6719	-0.0104	0.20953	82.96%
	t-stat	*22.36*	*8.54*	*-0.14*	*5.55*	
Q3	Coeff.	1.0765	0.5903	-0.1361	0.43096	84.43%
	t-stat	*19.54*	*6.64*	*-1.64*	*10.10*	
Highest Deviation	Coeff.	1.1010	0.2690	-0.1991	0.75229	81.51%
	t-stat	*15.14*	*2.29*	*-1.82*	*13.35*	

To summarize, the existence of positive and negative abnormal returns shows that the differences in riskiness as captured by the expected returns cannot account for the differences in excess returns across the deviation quartiles (Table 9). For the regressions in Table 12, the 4-factor expected returns even increase with deviation whereas the excess returns and the abnormal returns decrease; despite of their riskiness, firms in the highest-deviation quartile have the lowest excess return. As a consequence, differences in abnormal returns between highest- and lowest-deviation quartile portfolios are even greater than the differences in excess returns.

5.4.2 The role of size

There are several reasons why size could be a determinant of the abnormal performance of IPO stocks. First, the coefficients on the size factor in Table 12 show a pattern that could be interpreted such that small firms are overrepresented in the highest-deviation portfolio. Second, as documented in prior literature (and also shown here), broad equal-weighted portfolios of IPO firms show a tendency to earn negative abnormal returns, whereas there is no such finding for value-weighted IPO portfolios. The finding of underperformance for equal-weighted portfolios might reflect a bad model problem for small firms in general. Fama (1998) raises the concern that all asset pricing models deliver a bad description of tiny firms' expected returns. Brav and Gompers (1997) and Brav et al. (2000) empirical results support his hypothesis. They generalize the underperformance phenomenon from an IPO phenomenon to a small-firms phenomenon. Furthermore, Fama and French (1993) show that there is a monotonic trend in the intercepts of the 3-factor model for low-BM firms. Small firms in this group show a negative abnormal return, big firms a positive abnormal return. Mitchell and Stafford (2000) find a similar abnormal return pattern in their sample of SEO firms. Thus, differences between small and big firms' abnormal returns and the associated significance level are potentially overstated by a bad model for low-BM firms.

To test whether the size effect interacts with the explanation regarding information risk, I split my sample simultaneously into quartiles of size and deviation, where size is the beginning-of-month market capitalization.[49] The simultaneous splitting does not assure an even distribution of all firms in a given month over the 16 size-deviation portfolios, hence I maintain the requirement of at least three firms in a given month to form a calendar-time portfolio.[50]

49 One might worry about using market capitalization in a setting where prices are in a correction process. I therefore perform the same analysis using total assets as size variable. Results are similar to using beginning market capitalization as size measure. Note that this test is only economically meaningful for equal-weighted portfolios

50 Applying the Mitchell and Stafford (2000) requirement of 10 firms in each of the monthly 16

The number of months in the returns series drops, compared to the univariate sample split, in particular for portfolios with only one year holding period (this portfolio loses 45 monthly observations). Similar to the previous tables for the deviation variable, I add the returns series for the portfolio that is long in smallest firms and short in biggest firms to allow the assessment of the statistical significance of the difference, separately for each deviation quartile.

Regressions are run on the value- and equal-weighted portfolio returns and use the 3-factor (Panels A) and the 4-factor model (Panels B) as benchmarks.[51] Table 13 presents the abnormal returns on value-weighted portfolios from different holding periods. Note that the approach ensures that the month series is the same for all portfolios for a given holding period. Starting from the biggest-/lowest-deviation portfolio, there is a decline in intercepts along both dimensions, size and deviation. This decline is monotonic except for the respective extreme quartiles with the expectedly lowest abnormal returns. More importantly, the differences between the extreme categories are comparable. For the first table in Panel B, for example, the abnormal return estimate for the 'High-low' portfolio in the big firms quartile is -2.61% versus -2.66% for the 'Small-Big' portfolio in the lowest-deviation quartile. The differences decline from big to small firms and from low- to high-deviation firms. This pattern is similar in the entire table. It should be noted that the difference becomes insignificant in the group of smallest firms and in the highest-deviation group; thus, the respective effect (size or deviation) dominates the other only in the quartiles with extreme negative abnormal returns. Deviation looses its explanatory power for the smallest size quartile and, conversely, size looses its explanatory power in the highest-deviation quartile.

The main conclusions from this analysis are supported by the results of the 3-factor regression as displayed in Panel A. While results are similar, positive abnormal returns are generally slightly lower, negative abnormal returns slightly higher compared to the 3-factor model. As a consequence, the abnormal returns on the return differences are smaller and slightly less significant. Fama and French (1993) show that 3-factor regressions yield a monotonic pattern in intercepts when applied to low-book-to-market firms, such as IPOs. Specifically, they show that, in the lowest-BM quintile of their sample, small firms significantly underperform and big firms outperform the 3-factor model. To the extent that their results can be generalized to hold true for my tests,

portfolios lets the sample of months drop substantially to 127 (197, 246) months for the '1 Year' ('2 Year', '3 Year') portfolio. Despite the diminished sample size, significance levels remain high; results for both value- and equal-weighted portfolios are unaffected.

51 The results of the GARCH specification as well as for equal-weighted portfolios lead to similar conclusions and are therefore presented in the appendix only. See Tables A.5, A.6 and A.7.

one could expect to find a significant difference between small and big firms, partially induced by the asset pricing models.

Overall, there is under- and overperformance among the biggest firms, depending on the deviation and there is also under- and overperformance among the lowest-deviation firms, depending on size. The differences between extreme quartiles are generally significant. I conclude from this analysis that the size effect and the deviation explanation co-exist.

Table 13: Abnormal Value-Weighted Portfolio Returns per Deviation and Size Quartiles (OLS)

The sample of IPO firms is simultaneously split into deviation and size quartiles; the double-sorting leads to sixteen portfolios each calendar month with at least three firms. The table displays abnormal returns on these sixteen time series. Additionally, in the 'Small - Big' category, abnormal returns on the returns differences between small and big stocks are reported for each deviation quartile: Conversely, the 'High - Low' row contains abnormal returns on the returns differences between highest-deviation and lowest-deviation firms. Panel A presents 3-factor abnormal returns, Panel B contains the 4-factor abnormal returns.

Panel A: 3-factor abnormal returns

'1 Year' portfolio time-series (236 months)

	Big		Q2		Q3		Small		Small - Big	
Deviation Quartile	Abnormal Return	t-stat	Abnormal Return	t-stat	Abnormal Return	t-stat	Abnormal Return	t-stat	Abnormal Return	t-stat
Lowest	1.27%	3.19	0.46%	1.20	0.51%	1.14	-1.32%	-2.54	-2.59%	-3.92
Q2	0.84%	2.36	0.39%	0.98	0.00%	-0.01	-0.49%	-1.00	-1.33%	-2.13
Q3	-0.09%	-0.21	-0.29%	-0.81	-0.40%	-0.94	-1.39%	-2.77	-1.30%	-2.19
Highest	-1.09%	-2.18	-1.23%	-2.56	-1.12%	-2.17	-2.21%	-3.65	-1.13%	-1.61
High - Low	-2.35%	-3.76	-1.69%	-2.87	-1.62%	-2.54	-0.89%	-1.11		

'2 Year' portfolio time-series (270 months)

	Big		Q2		Q3		Small		Small - Big	
Deviation Quartile	Abnormal Return	t-stat	Abnormal Return	t-stat	Abnormal Return	t-stat	Abnormal Return	t-stat	Abnormal Return	t-stat
Lowest	1.10%	3.81	0.14%	0.56	-0.44%	-1.48	-1.36%	-3.06	-2.45%	-4.38
Q2	0.30%	1.06	-0.06%	-0.23	-0.77%	-2.32	-1.30%	-3.14	-1.60%	-3.11
Q3	-0.18%	-0.60	-0.78%	-2.81	-0.87%	-2.50	-0.93%	-2.05	-0.75%	-1.44
Highest	-0.95%	-2.15	-1.11%	-2.91	-1.17%	-2.76	-1.60%	-2.86	-0.66%	-1.06
High - Low	-2.04%	-3.88	-1.25%	-3.04	-0.74%	-1.58	-0.25%	-0.46		

'3 Year' portfolio time-series (274 months)

	Big		Q2		Q3		Small		Small - Big	
Deviation Quartile	Abnormal Return	t-stat	Abnormal Return	t-stat	Abnormal Return	t-stat	Abnormal Return	t-stat	Abnormal Return	t-stat
Lowest	0.84%	3.31	0.23%	0.93	-0.32%	-1.02	-0.59%	-1.24	-1.43%	-2.45
Q2	0.30%	1.39	-0.23%	-1.06	-0.90%	-2.81	-0.83%	-2.20	-1.13%	-2.55
Q3	0.05%	0.19	-0.72%	-2.67	-0.66%	-2.05	-0.62%	-1.32	-0.68%	-1.23
Highest	-0.45%	-1.20	-0.91%	-2.66	-1.23%	-2.86	-0.93%	-1.67	-0.48%	-0.81
High - Low	-1.29%	-2.80	-1.14%	-2.98	-0.91%	-2.41	-0.34%	-0.72		

Panel B: 4-factor abnormal returns

'1 Year' portfolio time-series (236 months)

	Big		Q2		Q3		Small		Small - Big	
Deviation Quartile	Abnormal Return	t-stat	Abnormal Return	t-stat	Abnormal Return	t-stat	Abnormal Return	t-stat	Abnormal Return	t-stat
Lowest	1.36%	3.42	0.55%	1.47	0.54%	1.22	-1.30%	-2.49	-2.66%	-4.01
Q2	0.86%	2.40	0.43%	1.08	-0.05%	-0.14	-0.68%	-1.43	-1.54%	-2.53
Q3	-0.22%	-0.51	-0.41%	-1.17	-0.61%	-1.50	-1.73%	-3.84	-1.51%	-2.60
Highest	-1.26%	-2.59	-1.48%	-3.31	-1.44%	-3.07	-2.71%	-5.47	-1.46%	-2.19
High - Low	-2.61%	-4.33	-2.04%	-3.79	-1.98%	-3.35	-1.41%	-1.97		

'2 Year' portfolio time-series (270 months)

	Big		Q2		Q3		Small		Small - Big	
Deviation Quartile	Abnormal Return	t-stat	Abnormal Return	t-stat	Abnormal Return	t-stat	Abnormal Return	t-stat	Abnormal Return	t-stat
Lowest	1.17%	4.12	0.17%	0.65	-0.48%	-1.61	-1.59%	-3.80	-2.76%	-5.28
Q2	0.31%	1.12	-0.09%	-0.33	-0.90%	-2.80	-1.59%	-4.35	-1.91%	-4.05
Q3	-0.25%	-0.85	-0.89%	-3.30	-1.09%	-3.46	-1.26%	-3.21	-1.01%	-2.05
Highest	-1.10%	-2.55	-1.31%	-3.69	-1.52%	-4.28	-2.15%	-5.10	-1.05%	-1.87
High - Low	-2.27%	-4.48	-1.48%	-3.85	-1.04%	-2.49	-0.56%	-1.13		

'3 Year' portfolio time-series (274 months)

	Big		Q2		Q3		Small		Small - Big	
Deviation Quartile	Abnormal Return	t-stat	Abnormal Return	t-stat	Abnormal Return	t-stat	Abnormal Return	t-stat	Abnormal Return	t-stat
Lowest	0.88%	3.47	0.23%	0.93	-0.44%	-1.44	-0.92%	-2.18	-1.80%	-3.40
Q2	0.32%	1.51	-0.27%	-1.26	-1.08%	-3.65	-1.09%	-3.25	-1.41%	-3.55
Q3	0.00%	-0.02	-0.85%	-3.30	-0.88%	-3.09	-1.01%	-2.60	-1.01%	-2.00
Highest	-0.59%	-1.60	-1.13%	-3.68	-1.57%	-4.43	-1.45%	-3.41	-0.86%	-1.63
High - Low	-1.47%	-3.28	-1.36%	-3.87	-1.14%	-3.32	-0.53%	-1.17		

5.4.3 Analysis of subperiods

Splitting the time series of returns into subperiods serves several purposes. First, it allows the loadings in the asset pricing regression to change over time. Recall that the regression is run on a time-series of portfolio returns. Regression parameters are therefore assumed to be constant for the full time period. However, as Mitchell and Stafford (2000) point out, this may not be the case as the portfolio composition changes. Firms drop out and other firms are included each month. With this subperiod analysis, I alleviate some of this concern by allowing the regression coefficients to differ between subperiods.[52]

As seen in Table 3, many IPOs took place in the mid-nineties; comparatively few firms went public in the early eighties and after 1999. Thus, the test also addresses the concern of Loughran and Ritter (1995, 2000) that underperformance is concentrated in markets with high event occurrence. Their argument is based on an opportunity window for managers to detect and exploit investors' temporary willingness to overpay IPOs. The test in this section is able to detect potential differences between the four subperiods.

More directly, the subperiods allow for the detection of over-time patterns in the abnormal returns, but also in the explanatory power of the deviation variable. I hypothesize that the effect does not diminish over time. This is in contrast to the analysis of Teoh et al. (1998). They provide evidence that the causal relation between their explanation variable (abnormal discretionary current accruals) and negative abnormal returns is weak in the second half of their sample period.

The regressions are run separately for four subperiods of (almost) equal length; Table 14 summarizes the results for a holding period of two years. Each subperiod consists of 70 or 71 months of portfolio returns data, so the statistical power of the test decreases compared to the full sample period tests. In each subperiod, only one of the 3-factor abnormal returns is significant. Depending on the average abnormal performance of the full sample in the respective subperiod, either the positive abnormal return for the lowest-deviation quartile or the negative abnormal return for the highest-deviation quartile is significant. Nevertheless, the difference between high and low deviation quartiles remains economically big and statistically significant for all subperiods. I conclude that the explanatory power of the deviation does not decline over time (in fact, it is highest in the last subperiod).

---

52 This first issue is more directly addressed when firm-specific abnormal returns are employed in Section 6.1.

Table 14: Abnormal Value-Weighted Portfolio Returns per Calendar-Time Quartile

The table summarizes abnormal returns on the '2 Year' portfolio for different deviation quartiles and subperiods of equal length.

Panel A: 3-factor regression

	July1980 : Apr1986		May1986 : Mar1992		Apr1992 : Feb1998		Mar1998 : Dec2003	
Deviation Quartile	Abnormal Return	t-stat	Abnormal Return	t-stat	Abnormal Return	t-stat	Abnormal Return	t-stat
Lowest	0.68%	1.31	0.97%	2.55	0.29%	0.75	1.26%	2.03
Q2	-0.57%	-1.06	0.28%	0.87	0.07%	0.30	0.14%	0.20
Q3	-0.62%	-1.44	0.03%	0.09	-0.39%	-1.02	-1.10%	-1.53
Highest	-1.61%	-2.63	-0.28%	-0.64	-1.09%	-2.45	-1.69%	-1.62
High - Low	-2.29%	-2.83	-1.25%	-2.38	-1.38%	-2.47	-2.95%	-2.26

Panel B: 4-factor regression

	July1980 : Apr1986		May1986 : Mar1992		Apr1992 : Feb1998		Mar1998 : Dec2003	
Deviation Quartile	Abnormal Return	t-stat	Abnormal Return	t-stat	Abnormal Return	t-stat	Abnormal Return	t-stat
Lowest	0.72%	1.30	0.99%	2.58	0.33%	0.86	1.67%	2.81
Q2	-0.37%	-0.66	0.27%	0.84	0.09%	0.39	0.23%	0.31
Q3	-0.35%	-0.78	-0.06%	-0.16	-0.39%	-1.01	-1.25%	-1.69
Highest	-0.95%	-1.58	-0.40%	-0.94	-1.29%	-3.25	-2.06%	-1.94
High - Low	-1.67%	-2.02	-1.39%	-2.74	-1.62%	-3.23	-3.73%	-2.94

6. Robustness Tests

6.1 Varying the calendar-time approach

The calendar-time approach as applied in the preceding sections assumes constant factor loadings over the estimation period. Jaffe (1974) and Mandelker (1974) propose to measure abnormal returns on a firm-specific basis and then form monthly calendar-time portfolios using abnormal returns. Mitchell and Stafford (2000) compare both calendar-time methods and conclude that there is no difference in inferences about abnormal returns, but the Jaffe and Mandelker variant generally leads to more conservative point estimates. Firm- and month-specific abnormal return are hard, if not impossible, to estimate using an asset pricing model. A potential solution is to lower the returns frequency down to daily data to get the necessary degrees of freedom, but 22 daily returns (on average) introduce too much noise to reliably estimate abnormal returns. Mitchell and Stafford therefore propose that one measures firm-specific abnormal returns over a certain post-event period using monthly data. As a consequence, the firm-specific loadings do not change from month to month (are not month-specific), but by revising the portfolio composition every month, the implicit loadings to estimate the abnormal return for this portfolio vary.

I apply this method to get firm-specific abnormal return estimates as follows. For each firm, I require at least 10 monthly return observations in the first three years after the issuance. This requirement reduces the sample by 542 to 5,596 firms. The abnormal portfolio return in a given month is the (equal- or value-weighted) average firm-specific abnormal return of all firms with an event in the last one to three years (i.e. the same portfolio inclusion rules as before apply). I still require at least 3 firms per month; the result of this procedure is a time series of abnormal portfolio returns for the same months as in the main tests of this work. The grand mean and the variance of this time series of monthly averages can be used to assess the magnitude and the significance of these abnormal returns. Note that the abnormal returns measurement per se does not control for overlaps in the estimation period. Again, the cross-correlation problem is only overcome by the formation of monthly portfolios.

To control for heteroscedasticity in this setting, I follow the aforementioned articles by Jaffe, Mandelker, and Mitchell and Stafford and weight the monthly portfolio averages by their estimation precision. Specifically, the monthly mean abnormal returns are divided by the standard deviation of the firm-specific abnormal returns in a month. This leads to a time series of standardized means which is only used to estimate the significance level, labeled 't-stat (std.)' in the following tables. As the presented means are from the unweighted time series of abnormal portfolio returns, the signs of abnormal return and standardized test statistic might differ. For this reason, I also report the t-statistics from the unweighted series (which might be biased by the varying number of firms). Table 15 presents the mean abnormal returns for equal- and value-weighted portfolios per deviation quartile.

Significance levels generally increase compared to my main tests, hence, I conclude that the previous findings are robust to this change in methodology. Interestingly, the differences between equal- and value-weighting strategies are even more pronounced. In Panel A, only the lowest-deviation quartiles show positive abnormal returns, the other quartiles earn significantly negative abnormal returns. In the value-weighted results of Panel B, only the highest-deviation portfolio with a horizon of one year earns a negative abnormal return of -0.15% per month. The 4-factor abnormal returns in Table 16 show the same qualitative pattern. Individual estimates, however, are generally lower. Positive abnormal returns diminish only slightly, but negative estimates drop substantially. This indicates that firms with initially overestimated information risk are generally firms with good information quality. The augmentation of the asset pricing model hardly alters the expected return for these firms. In contrast, high-deviation firms, whose information risk has been underestimated, turn out to be firms with bad information quality. Their expected returns increase on average; the abnormal returns become even more negative. Consequently, the abnormal returns on the long-short portfolios are lower than their 3-factor equivalents. Independent of holding period and weighting scheme, the abnormal returns are all below -1.00% per month.

6.2 Firm-specific tests

While all prior tests are on the portfolio level, the tests in this section will be on a firm-specific basis in order to give an impression on the cross-sectional variation of the deviation variable (Subsection 6.2.1) and the firm-specific abnormal return (Subsections 6.2.2 and 6.2.3). The price one pays is that firm-specific abnormal return estimates are generally noisier and less powerful than portfolio abnormal returns.

Table 15: Abnormal Portfolio Returns per Deviation Quartile – Jaffe-Mandelker Method (3-Factor)

This table reports grand means of portfolio abnormal returns. Portfolio abnormal returns are the equal- or value-weighted means of firm-specific abnormal returns. The abnormal returns estimates and the test statistic labeled 't-stat'are from the time series of unweighted monthly observations. The test statistic labeled 't-stat (std.)' is the significance from a time-series where the monthly observations are divided by the standard deviation of individual abnormal returns in the portfolio to control for heteroscedasticity.

Panel A: Average abnormal return on equal-weighted portfolios for deviation quartiles

	1 Year(281 months)			2 Years(282 months)			3 Years(282 months)		
Deviation Quartile	Abnormal Return	t-stat	t-stat (std.)	Abnormal Return	t-stat	t-stat (std.)	Abnormal Return	t-stat	t-stat (std.)
Lowest	0.33%	5.63	5.83	0.22%	5.42	5.55	0.15%	4.20	4.51
Q2	-0.27%	-5.52	-3.83	-0.41%	-11.99	-9.91	-0.37%	-11.21	-10.57
Q3	-0.41%	-8.77	-7.18	-0.44%	-12.46	-10.20	-0.55%	-17.01	-13.49
Highest	-0.70%	-12.07	-13.20	-0.71%	-16.49	-17.37	-0.63%	-18.16	-18.94
High - Low	-1.03%	-15.01	-15.73	-0.93%	-19.48	-19.23	-0.78%	-22.63	-21.05

Panel B: Average abnormal return on value-weighted portfolios for deviation quartiles

	1 Year(281 months)			2 Years(282 months)			3 Years(282 months)		
Deviation Quartile	Abnormal Return	t-stat	t-stat (std.)	Abnormal Return	t-stat	t-stat (std.)	Abnormal Return	t-stat	t-stat (std.)
Lowest	1.12%	15.50	11.13	1.35%	22.38	17.10	1.51%	25.49	19.75
Q2	0.53%	8.94	6.96	0.62%	13.26	12.42	0.71%	14.60	14.76
Q3	0.20%	3.32	1.74	0.27%	5.22	2.26	0.32%	5.96	2.20
Highest	-0.15%	-1.88	-4.94	0.34%	3.92	-0.98	0.66%	7.41	2.01
High - Low	-1.27%	-12.37	-10.18	-1.01%	-11.30	-10.81	-0.84%	-10.02	-10.18

Table 16: Abnormal Portfolio Returns per Deviation Quartile – Jaffe-Mandelker Method (4-Factor)

This table presents 4-factor abnormal returns. For a detailed description, see Table 15.

Panel A: Average abnormal return on equal-weighted portfolios for deviation quartiles

Deviation Quartile	1 Year(281 months) Abnormal Return	t-stat	t-stat (std.)	2 Years(282 months) Abnormal Return	t-stat	t-stat (std.)	3 Years(282 months) Abnormal Return	t-stat	t-stat (std.)
Lowest	0.20%	2.98	4.23	0.11%	2.24	3.09	0.04%	0.86	1.99
Q2	-0.41%	-7.65	-5.62	-0.59%	-15.12	-13.90	-0.53%	-16.48	-15.74
Q3	-0.68%	-12.02	-11.63	-0.70%	-14.82	-14.72	-0.77%	-18.38	-19.24
Highest	-1.09%	-12.62	-15.10	-1.12%	-16.82	-20.15	-1.00%	-18.49	-22.43
High - Low	-1.29%	-12.98	-14.12	-1.22%	-15.46	-15.86	-1.04%	-17.18	-17.04

Panel B: Average abnormal return on value-weighted portfolios for deviation quartiles

Deviation Quartile	1 Year(281 months) Abnormal Return	t-stat	t-stat (std.)	2 Years(282 months) Abnormal Return	t-stat	t-stat (std.)	3 Years(282 months) Abnormal Return	t-stat	t-stat (std.)
Lowest	1.12%	13.26	9.18	1.39%	19.13	13.92	1.55%	22.77	16.44
Q2	0.48%	8.12	6.28	0.59%	13.86	13.26	0.72%	15.51	16.30
Q3	0.12%	1.64	2.40	0.22%	3.98	3.59	0.32%	5.86	4.52
Highest	-0.36%	-4.28	-4.63	0.16%	1.94	0.13	0.48%	6.50	3.92
High - Low	-1.48%	-11.54	-9.31	-1.23%	-10.81	-9.49	-1.07%	-11.12	-8.96

6.2.1 Deviation and IPO firm characteristics

Although news on new firms are scarce, one might assume that the over- and underestimation is also a function of the stability of the firm's business environment and also of the firm's stage in the lifecycle. Specifically, I hypothesize older firms to be well established in their environment and to be closer to steady state than younger firms. The absolute value of the deviation variable is therefore presumably smaller (the deviation is closer to zero) for older firms. Note that the deviation captures the surprise in the information riskiness of the newly public firm. The lack of possibilities to assess this information risk will still dominate the influence of firm age. One cannot expect a large portion of the deviation being explained by age as still no prior information is available. The stability of the firm's business (for which I proxy with firm age), however, could lead to a higher congruence of the information in the offering prospectus to reported performance figures in the future. I test the relation of the deviation variable and the IPO firm's age in a univariate regression of the following form:

$$Abs(Deviation_j) = \lambda_0 + \lambda_1 FirmAge_j + \epsilon_j \tag{13}$$

Firm age is defined as the year of the IPO less the founding year.[53] The sample for this test is reduced to a subset of 4,661 IPO firms for which founding years are available. The mean (median) age in this sample is 14 (7) years. This figure might contradict the common belief that only extremely young firms go public where information asymmetry is very high. Thus, it is not strange that I find underestimation and overestimation of information risk at the offering date for 3,003 and 3,135 firms of the sample, respectively.

Additionally, one might assume that the firm's disclosure is more comprehensive, the larger the dollar volume of the offering. In the case of a large offer volume, more investors have to be convinced of the firm to actually place buy orders.[54] Therefore, the information risk might be easier to assess. Thus, I also hypothesize that the absolute deviation is smaller for larger offerings. To control for the effect of firm size, I also include the firm's market capitalization in the month of first listing.

---

[53] This data is described in Loughran and Ritter (2004) and available on Jay Ritter's website, http://bear.cba.ufl.edu/ritter/ipodata.htm.

[54] According to Ritter (2002), road shows are only held for invited institutional investors. Information dissemination is thus limited to this circle with an informational disadvantage for private investors. In contrast, if a substantial part of the shareholder potential consists of private investors, mass media might be more appropriate. This should, ceteris paribus, reduce the information asymmetry between shareholder groups.

Table 17: Firm Age Regressions

This table presents regressions of firm age, offer volume and market capitalization on the absolute value of the deviation variable. The sample size is 4,661 firms for which founding years are available.

	Intercept	Firm Age	Offer Volume	MktCap	Adj. R^2
Coefficient	0.4207	-0.0016	-	-	0.82%
t-stat	*67.66*	*-6.30*			
Coefficient	0.4221	-0.0014	-0.0001	-	0.96%
t-stat	*67.70*	*-5.56*	*-2.73*		
Coefficient	0.4224	-0.0015	-	-0.0000	0.89%
t-stat	*67.34*	*-5.99*		*-1.99*	
Coefficient	0.4224	-0.0014	-0.0001	-0.0000	0.94%
t-stat	*67.36*	*-5.56*	*-1.91*	*-0.38*	

$$Abs(Deviation_j) = \lambda_0 + \lambda_1 FirmAge_j + \epsilon_j \quad (14)$$

$$Abs(Deviation_j) = \lambda_0 + \lambda_1 FirmAge_j + \lambda_2 OfferVolume_j + \epsilon_j \quad (15)$$

$$Abs(Deviation_j) = \lambda_0 + \lambda_1 FirmAge_j + \lambda_2 MktCap_j + \epsilon_j \quad (16)$$

$$Abs(Deviation_j) = \lambda_0 + \lambda_1 FirmAge_j + \lambda_2 OfferVolume_j + \lambda_3 MktCap_j + \epsilon_j \quad (17)$$

Table 17 summarizes the regression results. As expected, the conditional mean λ_0 is positive (0.42) and highly significant across all specifications. Firm age has only a limited reducing effect on the deviation variable of -0.0016 per year, but it is significant (t = 6.30). This finding is consistent with the hypothesis that the misestimation is smaller for more stable firms. In separate regressions, the coefficients both on offer volume and market capitalization are negative.[55] But when included in the same regression, the explanatory power of market capitalization shrinks; while the coefficient remains very small, it is no longer significant at conventional levels. The coefficient on offer volume, however, also remains unaffected and is still significant (t = -1.91). A higher offer volume is associated with a lower (absolute) deviation from the true

[55] Data on offer volume is obtained from the SDC database.

firm-specific information risk. This evidence supports the hypothesis of larger offers requiring more disclosure and therefore allowing for a more accurate assessment of the firm's information risk, over and above the impact of firm age.

6.2.2 Firm-specific abnormal return and size

The Jaffe-Mandelker tests establish that the deviation variable can also be used to test for differences in firm-specific abnormal returns. Thus, the main purpose of introducing firm-specific abnormal returns at this point is to link the previous findings to changes in the firm's size and operating performance. The relation of firm-specific abnormal returns and size can be clarified in this setting by a bivariate regression:

$$\alpha_j^{3f/4f} = \lambda_0 + \lambda_1 DevDummy_j + \epsilon_j \quad (18)$$

$$\alpha_j^{3f/4f} = \lambda_0 + \lambda_1 DevDummy_j + \lambda_2 MktCap_j + \epsilon_j \quad (19)$$

I use firm-specific abnormal return as dependent variable despite of the overlap in estimation period. As Mitchell and Stafford (2000) discuss, the overlap does not lead to biased estimates, but only the significance of these estimates may be overstated. The measure of size, *MktCap*, is the market capitalization of the first month with returns data available on CRSP. Consistent with its non-parametric role as a directional indicator and quartile separator, I transform the deviation variable into a dummy, *DevDummy*, which takes on the value of 1, when the deviation is positive, and 0 if not. A positive deviation signals an initial underestimation of the firm's information risk such that one would expect a lower abnormal return. The results of this very low-powered regression, presented in Table 18, show that this is indeed the case, the deviation dummy loads negatively. Conversely, size is positively associated with abnormal returns. Both coefficients are significant at the 0.01 level. As lowest (highest) deviation firms are on average good (bad) information quality firms, one might have expected that the deviation dummy loads more negatively when 4-factor abnormal returns serve as dependent variable. These results confirm the finding in the calendar-time portfolio tests (Section 5.4.2), that both size and the deviation have (incremental) explanatory power for abnormal returns.

Table 18: Size Regressions

The table displays regression results on firm-specific 3-factor and 4-factor abnormal returns. *DevDummy* is the dummy variable which is zero for negative deviations and 1 for positive deviations, *MktCap* is the market capitalization in the first month with return data on CRSP. The sample consists of 5,596 firms for which firm-specific abnormal return estimates are attainable.

Panel A: 3-factor abnormal returns

	Intercept	DevDummy	MktCap	Adj. R^2
Coefficient	-0.0003	-0.0056	-	0.30%
t-stat	*-0.28*	*-4.25*		
Coefficient	-0.0007	-0.0057	0.0000	0.43%
t-stat	*-0.74*	*-4.33*	*2.86*	

Panel B: 4-factor abnormal returns

	Intercept	DevDummy	MktCap	Adj. R^2
Coefficient	-0.0016	-0.0088	-	0.65%
t-stat	*-1.62*	*-6.15*		
Coefficient	-0.0020	-0.0089	0.0000	0.74%
t-stat	*-1.98*	*-6.22*	*2.38*	

6.2.3 Firm-specific abnormal return and operating performance

So far, the work has only been concerned about a denominator effect in the valuation equation. The explanation does not rule out, however, that changes in the operating performance (earnings growth) over the regarded period cause the price adjustments. The argument somewhat resembles the argument in Teoh et al. (1998). As they focus on accruals reversal, their argument is restricted to predicting post-issue underperformance, whereas a positive development in earnings explicitly allows for the possibility of a positive abnormal return. It is generally held true that the 3-factor model captures operating performance and operating risks fairly well, nevertheless I combine deviation and operating performance in one regression to disentangle numerator and denominator effects:

$$\alpha_j^{3f/4f} = \lambda_0 + \lambda_1 DevDummy_j + \epsilon_j \quad (20)$$

$$\alpha_j^{3f/4f} = \lambda_0 + \lambda_1 DevDummy_j + \lambda_2 OpPerf_j + \epsilon_j \quad (21)$$

$$\alpha_j^{3f/4f} = \lambda_0 + \lambda_1 DevDummy_j + \lambda_2 OpPerf_j + \lambda_3 MktCap_j + \epsilon_j \quad (22)$$

α_j is firm j's abnormal return estimate from a 3-factor or 4-factor regression, $DevDummy_j$ denotes the dummy variable which has a value of one for positive deviations, and $OpPerf_j$ is the average change in net income before extraordinary items over the same three years as used to estimate the abnormal return, scaled by the market capitalization variable, $MktCap_j$, as defined above. If earnings data was not available for some years, the average consists of less than three change figures. As some of the 5,596 firms with abnormal returns did not have at least two consecutive earnings figures on Compustat within this period, the sample reduces to 5,015 firms.

As expected from the preceding results, the deviation dummy loads negatively regardless of whether the 3-factor or the 4-factor model abnormal return serves as dependent variable. The coefficients also confirm that abnormal returns and the operating performance are positively related in both panels. The higher the (scaled) average change over the first 36 months after listing, the higher is the abnormal return. The association with the deviation variable does not decrease (but slightly increase) when operating performance is included as an additional independent variable. Although loading significantly, adding the market capitalization has virtually no effect over adding the operating performance.

Note that my measure for operating performance (the realized average change in earnings) can only be assessed ex-post. Thus, it is not surprising that, with hindsight, operating performance is positively associated with abnormal returns. The important result from these tests is that the loading on the deviation dummy does not change meaningfully after the inclusion of operating performance, but, in fact, remains highly significant.

6.3 Further Robustness Tests

To mitigate the concern that only a few firms drive the underperformance, I only use firm-month observations with more than \$50 million market capitalization to form calendar-time portfolios. Conversely, I delete observations with more than \$1 billion such that big firms cannot drive the overperformance of value-weighted lowest-deviation quartile portfolios. The conclusions from the main test results about the monotonic

Table 19: Operating Performance Regressions

The table displays regression results on firm-specific 3-factor and 4-factor abnormal returns. *DevDummy* is the dummy variable which is zero for negative deviations and 1 for positive deviations, *OpPerf* is the average change in net income before extraordinary items in the first three years after the issuance and *MktCap* is the market capitalization in the first month with return data on CRSP. The sample reduces to 4,899 firms for which firm-specific abnormal return estimates and operating performance data are attainable.

Panel A: 3-factor abnormal return as dependent variable

	Intercept	DevDummy	OpPerf	MktCap	Adj. R^2
Coefficient	0.0016	-0.0041	-	-	0.20%
t-stat	*1.83*	*-3.36*			
Coefficient	0.0017	-0.0042	0.0039	-	0.43%
t-stat	*1.93*	*-3.44*	*3.53*		
Coefficient	0.0013	-0.0043	0.0039	0.0000	0.54%
t-stat	*1.49*	*-3.51*	*3.53*	*2.54*	

Panel B: 4-factor abnormal return as dependent variable

	Intercept	DevDummy	OpPerf	MktCap	Adj. R^2
Coefficient	0.0005	-0.0068	-	-	0.54%
t-stat	*0.58*	*-5.30*			
Coefficient	0.0006	-0.0069	0.0040	-	0.74%
t-stat	*0.67*	*-5.38*	*3.37*		
Coefficient	0.0003	-0.0070	0.0040	0.0000	0.82%
t-stat	*0.30*	*-5.45*	*3.37*	*2.22*	

patterns across quartiles and investment horizons remain the same. In particular, both truncated samples show significant differences between the extreme deviation quartiles.

In a further robustness test, I change the estimation period over which the firm-specific e-loadings are estimated. So far, I have used all trading days in the first year after the issuance. This number is not equal across firms, but ranges from 100 (the minimum requirement) to 253 days. The approach potentially leads to more accurate estimates for firms with more trading days. Addressing this issue, I also calculate factor loadings using only the required number of 100 trading days in the first year. Shortening the estimation period introduces noise in the estimation. The difference between the extreme quartiles is still significant over all three investment horizons.

In a second test along these lines, I estimate e-loadings over the first six months after the IPO requiring at least 30 trading days. To test if an investment strategy on the deviation variable is generally implementable, I mimic investing in value- and equal-weighted IPO firm portfolios in Month 7 after the issuance. The holding periods for the individual stocks are until Month 12, 18, 24 and 30 (0.5, 1, 1.5 and 2 years). The sample of portfolio return observations is reduced to 276 months, only the half-year sample consists of 277 months.

Table 20 summarizes the results for the differences between the highest- and lowest-deviation quartile which is significant across all specifications. Consistent with the main test results, three patterns emerge: Value-weighted portfolios show a larger difference than equal-weighted portfolios and 4-factor differences are larger than 3-factor differences. Finally, the magnitude of the difference decreases with increasing investment horizon.

Table 20: Significance of the Difference Between Highest- and Lowest-Deviation Quartiles

The table displays OLS regression results on 3-factor and 4-factor portfolio returns where the portfolio is long in the highest- and short in the lowest-deviation quartile of firms. 'EW' ('VW') indicates that the respective quartile portfolios are equal-weighted (value-weighted). Deviation is measured with e-loadings gained over the first six months after the offering. The investment starts in Month 7. Sample sizes are in parentheses.

Panel A: 3-Factor Abnormal Returns

	Months 7 - 12 (277 months)		Months 7 - 18 (276 months)		Months 7 - 24 (276 months)		Months 7 - 30 (276 months)	
Difference High-low for	Abnormal Return	t-stat	Abnormal Return	t-stat	Abnormal Return	t-stat	Abnormal Return	t-stat
EW portfolios	-1.21%	-2.90	-0.92%	-3.10	-0.68%	-2.47	-0.52%	-1.94
VW portfolios	-1.42%	-2.46	-1.12%	-2.40	-0.89%	-2.19	-0.71%	-1.88

Panel B: 4-Factor Abnormal Returns

	Months 7 - 12 (277 months)		Months 7 - 18 (276 months)		Months 7 - 24 (276 months)		Months 7 - 30 (276 months)	
Difference High-low for	Abnormal Return	t-stat	Abnormal Return	t-stat	Abnormal Return	t-stat	Abnormal Return	t-stat
EW portfolios	-1.46%	-3.83	-1.03%	-3.54	-0.77%	-2.89	-0.62%	-2.42
VW portfolios	-1.60%	-2.83	-1.22%	-2.65	-1.00%	-2.47	-0.79%	-2.12

7. Concluding Remarks

This work links information risk to the long-term abnormal performance of IPO firms. As information risk is priced by investors, but cannot be assessed ex-ante for an IPO, investors in IPO firms have to form an expectation. Depending on whether the information risk has been initially underestimated (overestimated), the stock price has to be corrected downward (upward) as more and more firm-specific information becomes available. This gradual correction process leads to the appearance of abnormal returns (i.e., returns not explained by equilibrium asset pricing models) over a lengthy period.

Consistent with Bayesian theory, the updating process is unlikely to take place over a short period. First, young firms have high information risk in general; information about these firms is thus of relatively low credibility. Second, updating the prior requires a sufficient amount of new information which is only disseminated over a lengthy period. Overall, while the debate to date has focused on the existence of underperformance for the average IPO, this study presents an explanation for the full cross-sectional variation in IPO abnormal returns.

Information risk is empirically operationalized by earnings quality. Specifically, prior literature has established that accruals quality is the most comprehensive metric in capturing the notion of information risk. Traditional earnings quality metrics (including accruals quality), however, cannot be employed in my IPO setting because of stringent data requirements and mechanical dependence of observations over time; that is, changes in earnings quality are not adequately captured by existing metrics. Firm- and year-specific loadings on an accruals quality mimicking factor in an asset pricing regression, e-loadings, alleviate these shortcomings, as shown in the construct validity tests.

The average of all e-loadings in an industry serves as proxy for the expected value of an IPO's information risk. Over the first year after the listing, IPO-firm-specific e-loadings are calculated. The difference between firm-specific realized information risk and the expected value is the deviation variable. This deviation indicates whether the IPO firm's information risk has initially been underestimated or overestimated at the time of the offering. If information risk was underestimated (overestimated) and has to be corrected upward (downward), the expected return of this stock will increase (decrease) and stock prices will fall (rise) relative to the benchmark. Consistent with the average information risk being correctly estimated, there is little or no indication of average abnormal return in my IPO sample. However, I hypothesize and find a significant difference in abnormal returns between high-deviation firms and low-deviation firms. This difference declines with increasing investment horizons, consistent with the correction process gradually becoming more complete. This result is robust to sensitivity analyses using firm-specific abnormal returns, different asset pricing models and various estimation techniques. It is also shown not to be captured by a size effect and does not diminish over my sample period.

Appendix

Figure A.1: Abnormal Portfolio Returns for Rolling Short Investment Horizons (GARCH)

For a description, refer to Figure 1 in Section 5.3.

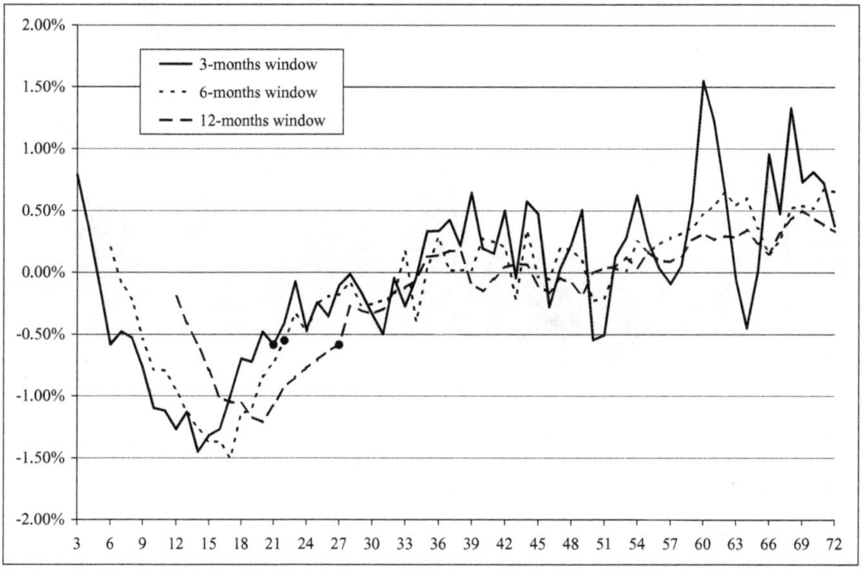

Figure A.2: Abnormal Portfolio Returns for Rolling Short Investment Horizons (4-factor) (GARCH)

For a description, refer to Figure 2 in Section 5.3.

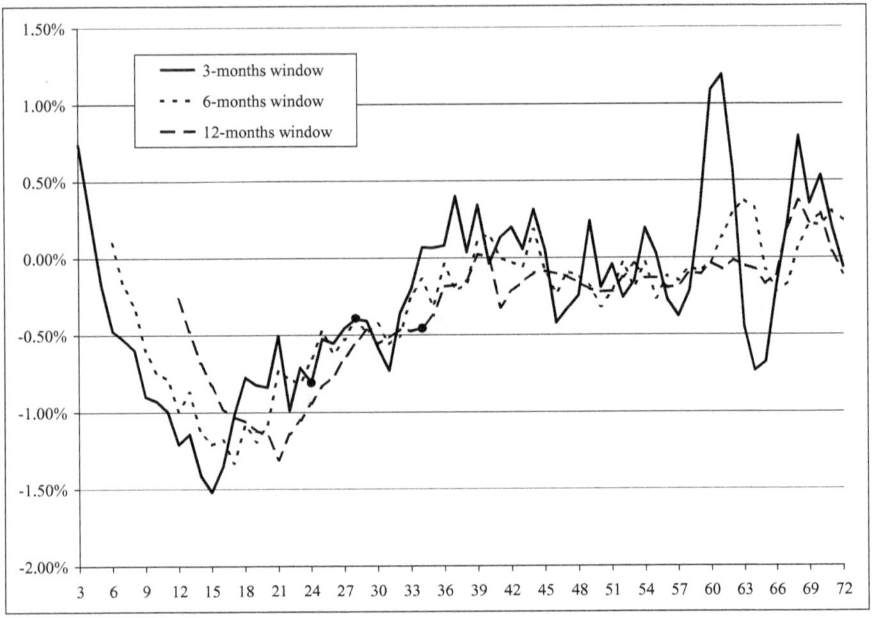

Table A.1: Abnormal Portfolio Returns for Rolling Short Investment Horizons (3-factor)

This table presents the 3-factor abnormal returns of equal-weighted portfolios. The column labeled '# Obs.' contains the number of monthly portfolios in the sample. 'T-stat' shows the test statistic associated with the abnormal return estimates, and 'p-value' is the corresponding (degrees-of-freedom-adjusted) probability value of the estimate being different from zero. Panel A contains the data for Figure 1, Panel B for Figure A.1.

Panel A: 3-factor model intercepts (OLS)

	3-months window				6-months window				12-months window			
End month	# Obs.	Abnormal Return	t-stat	p-value	# Obs.	Abnormal Return	t-stat	p-value	# Obs.	Abnormal Return	t-stat	p-value
3	261	0.62%	2.01	0.05								
4	261	0.23%	0.85	0.39								
5	261	-0.20%	-0.82	0.41								
6	261	-0.58%	-2.39	0.02	275	0.10%	0.43	0.67				
7	261	-0.54%	-2.00	0.05	275	-0.16%	-0.72	0.47				
8	260	-0.54%	-2.13	0.03	275	-0.28%	-1.31	0.19				
9	260	-0.70%	-2.55	0.01	275	-0.57%	-2.59	0.01				
10	260	-0.97%	-3.42	0.00	275	-0.79%	-3.34	0.00				
11	260	-1.07%	-3.71	0.00	275	-0.83%	-3.46	0.00				
12	260	-1.39%	-4.52	0.00	275	-0.96%	-3.77	0.00	281	-0.31%	-1.51	0.13
13	257	-1.22%	-3.79	0.00	275	-1.08%	-4.26	0.00	281	-0.50%	-2.39	0.02
14	253	-1.42%	-4.65	0.00	274	-1.28%	-4.88	0.00	280	-0.69%	-3.30	0.00
15	252	-1.37%	-4.37	0.00	273	-1.34%	-4.83	0.00	279	-0.82%	-3.81	0.00
16	250	-1.33%	-4.00	0.00	272	-1.39%	-4.92	0.00	278	-1.00%	-4.45	0.00
17	250	-1.16%	-3.41	0.00	271	-1.46%	-5.08	0.00	277	-1.06%	-4.60	0.00
18	249	-0.78%	-2.22	0.03	270	-1.26%	-4.29	0.00	276	-1.06%	-4.33	0.00

End month	3-months window				6-months window				12-months window			
	# Obs.	Abnormal Return	t-stat	p-value	# Obs.	Abnormal Return	t-stat	p-value	# Obs.	Abnormal Return	t-stat	p-value
19	248	-0.60%	-1.67	0.10	269	-1.12%	-3.80	0.00	275	-1.13%	-4.47	0.00
20	246	-0.52%	-1.42	0.16	268	-1.04%	-3.38	0.00	274	-1.18%	-4.54	0.00
21	244	-0.72%	-1.87	0.06	267	-0.86%	-2.67	0.01	273	-1.13%	-4.15	0.00
22	241	-0.45%	-1.26	0.21	266	-0.73%	-2.29	0.02	272	-1.09%	-3.99	0.00
23	240	-0.48%	-1.37	0.17	265	-0.54%	-1.68	0.09	271	-1.06%	-3.85	0.00
24	240	-0.74%	-2.18	0.03	264	-0.67%	-2.13	0.03	270	-0.96%	-3.46	0.00
25	239	-0.46%	-1.41	0.16	263	-0.67%	-2.25	0.03	269	-0.87%	-3.15	0.00
26	238	-0.48%	-1.49	0.14	262	-0.64%	-2.24	0.03	268	-0.81%	-2.93	0.00
27	237	-0.01%	-0.03	0.98	260	-0.48%	-1.74	0.08	267	-0.59%	-2.12	0.03
28	237	-0.07%	-0.21	0.84	258	-0.38%	-1.36	0.18	266	-0.52%	-1.84	0.07
29	235	-0.17%	-0.46	0.64	257	-0.30%	-1.01	0.31	265	-0.40%	-1.43	0.15
30	234	-0.24%	-0.62	0.53	256	-0.19%	-0.61	0.54	264	-0.45%	-1.57	0.12
31	232	-0.38%	-0.97	0.33	256	-0.34%	-1.09	0.28	263	-0.49%	-1.76	0.08
32	230	-0.10%	-0.26	0.80	254	-0.07%	-0.21	0.84	262	-0.35%	-1.23	0.22
33	226	0.15%	0.38	0.71	251	0.00%	0.01	0.99	261	-0.29%	-1.01	0.31
34	225	0.51%	1.20	0.23	251	0.13%	0.36	0.72	259	-0.17%	-0.57	0.57
35	223	0.44%	1.13	0.26	250	0.11%	0.33	0.74	259	-0.08%	-0.28	0.78
36	222	0.45%	1.22	0.22	248	0.38%	1.13	0.26	258	0.09%	0.30	0.77
37	219	0.69%	1.83	0.07	245	0.58%	1.67	0.10	257	0.11%	0.35	0.73
38	218	0.53%	1.42	0.16	244	0.34%	1.08	0.28	256	0.15%	0.49	0.62
39	216	0.66%	1.63	0.11	243	0.37%	1.15	0.25	254	0.26%	0.80	0.43
40	215	0.41%	1.06	0.29	241	0.40%	1.27	0.21	254	0.33%	0.97	0.33
41	213	0.44%	1.09	0.28	240	0.36%	1.16	0.25	253	0.13%	0.43	0.66
42	210	0.61%	1.51	0.13	239	0.32%	0.98	0.33	252	0.21%	0.74	0.46
43	209	0.35%	0.86	0.39	238	0.24%	0.74	0.46	250	0.28%	0.98	0.33
44	207	0.80%	2.03	0.04	237	0.46%	1.44	0.15	248	0.29%	1.03	0.30
45	205	0.44%	1.25	0.21	236	0.34%	1.13	0.26	247	0.23%	0.85	0.40

End	3-months window				6-months window				12-months window			
month	# Obs.	Abnormal Return	t-stat	p-value	# Obs.	Abnormal Return	t-stat	p-value	# Obs.	Abnormal Return	t-stat	p-value
46	204	-0.02%	-0.06	0.95	233	0.17%	0.59	0.56	245	0.15%	0.56	0.57
47	203	-0.10%	-0.33	0.74	232	0.32%	1.08	0.28	244	0.18%	0.68	0.49
48	201	0.03%	0.10	0.92	232	0.16%	0.56	0.58	243	0.16%	0.61	0.54
49	199	0.67%	1.67	0.10	230	0.06%	0.21	0.83	242	0.15%	0.54	0.59
50	197	0.01%	0.02	0.98	228	-0.04%	-0.14	0.89	241	0.18%	0.65	0.51
51	190	0.26%	0.58	0.56	226	0.06%	0.18	0.86	240	0.19%	0.71	0.48
52	186	0.04%	0.10	0.92	225	0.27%	0.87	0.39	239	0.15%	0.58	0.56
53	182	0.25%	0.67	0.50	223	0.10%	0.30	0.76	238	0.21%	0.80	0.42
54	180	0.58%	1.51	0.13	222	0.28%	0.86	0.39	237	0.20%	0.78	0.44
55	179	0.31%	0.85	0.40	221	0.10%	0.35	0.73	236	0.13%	0.53	0.60
56	178	0.03%	0.09	0.93	220	0.14%	0.48	0.63	235	0.06%	0.24	0.81
57	178	-0.23%	-0.70	0.48	219	0.11%	0.39	0.69	234	0.09%	0.34	0.73
58	177	0.00%	0.01	0.99	218	0.21%	0.72	0.47	233	0.18%	0.70	0.49
59	175	0.73%	1.56	0.12	217	0.17%	0.55	0.59	232	0.20%	0.72	0.47
60	173	1.36%	2.76	0.01	216	0.24%	0.75	0.46	231	0.26%	0.94	0.35
61	170	1.29%	2.75	0.01	215	0.43%	1.29	0.20	230	0.21%	0.77	0.44
62	169	0.64%	1.66	0.10	214	0.50%	1.56	0.12	229	0.27%	1.03	0.31
63	168	-0.07%	-0.18	0.86	212	0.51%	1.54	0.12	228	0.20%	0.75	0.46
64	167	-0.34%	-0.81	0.42	211	0.43%	1.27	0.21	227	0.18%	0.67	0.50
65	167	-0.25%	-0.49	0.62	210	0.22%	0.67	0.51	226	0.06%	0.23	0.82
66	166	0.33%	0.61	0.55	209	0.11%	0.32	0.75	225	0.09%	0.33	0.74
67	164	0.55%	1.09	0.28	208	0.18%	0.53	0.59	224	0.24%	0.89	0.38
68	163	1.09%	2.65	0.01	207	0.44%	1.23	0.22	223	0.36%	1.30	0.20
69	162	0.69%	1.86	0.06	206	0.56%	1.66	0.10	222	0.44%	1.57	0.12
70	160	0.82%	1.99	0.05	205	0.62%	1.98	0.05	221	0.42%	1.49	0.14
71	159	0.66%	1.48	0.14	202	0.72%	2.37	0.02	220	0.34%	1.27	0.21
72	158	0.38%	0.85	0.40	201	0.60%	2.01	0.05	219	0.20%	0.76	0.45

Panel B: 3-factor model intercepts (GARCH (1,1))

End month	3-months window # Obs.	Abnormal Return	t-stat	p-value	6-months window # Obs.	Abnormal Return	t-stat	p-value	12-months window # Obs.	Abnormal Return	t-stat	p-value
3	261	0.79%	3.38	0.00								
4	261	0.38%	1.68	0.09								
5	261	-0.08%	-0.39	0.70								
6	261	-0.58%	-2.22	0.03	275	0.20%	1.18	0.24				
7	261	-0.48%	-2.05	0.04	275	-0.08%	-0.43	0.67				
8	260	-0.53%	-2.41	0.02	275	-0.22%	-1.28	0.20				
9	260	-0.77%	-3.70	0.00	275	-0.54%	-3.41	0.00				
10	260	-1.10%	-5.07	0.00	275	-0.79%	-4.84	0.00				
11	260	-1.12%	-4.41	0.00	275	-0.80%	-4.37	0.00				
12	260	-1.27%	-5.65	0.00	275	-0.95%	-5.16	0.00	281	-0.19%	-1.42	0.16
13	257	-1.13%	-5.14	0.00	275	-1.13%	-5.98	0.00	281	-0.41%	-3.08	0.00
14	253	-1.45%	-6.64	0.00	274	-1.26%	-6.78	0.00	280	-0.58%	-4.36	0.00
15	252	-1.32%	-7.42	0.00	273	-1.37%	-7.96	0.00	279	-0.79%	-6.14	0.00
16	250	-1.27%	-5.78	0.00	272	-1.37%	-6.94	0.00	278	-1.02%	-7.28	0.00
17	250	-1.00%	-4.23	0.00	271	-1.50%	-6.74	0.00	277	-1.05%	-7.16	0.00
18	249	-0.70%	-3.12	0.00	270	-1.15%	-6.99	0.00	276	-1.06%	-7.44	0.00
19	248	-0.72%	-3.05	0.00	269	-1.10%	-6.16	0.00	275	-1.17%	-8.67	0.00
20	246	-0.48%	-2.13	0.03	268	-0.84%	-5.33	0.00	274	-1.21%	-8.80	0.00
21	244	-0.59%	-2.45	0.01	267	-0.73%	-4.05	0.00	273	-1.08%	-7.83	0.00
22	241	-0.41%	-1.52	0.13	266	-0.55%	-3.10	0.00	272	-0.93%	-6.32	0.00
23	240	-0.08%	-0.26	0.79	265	-0.33%	-1.54	0.12	271	-0.85%	-5.53	0.00
24	240	-0.46%	-1.71	0.09	264	-0.48%	-2.08	0.04	270	-0.78%	-5.45	0.00
25	239	-0.24%	-1.01	0.31	263	-0.25%	-1.14	0.25	269	-0.71%	-4.75	0.00

End	3-months window				6-months window				12-months window			
month	# Obs.	Abnormal Return	t-stat	p-value	# Obs.	Abnormal Return	t-stat	p-value	# Obs.	Abnormal Return	t-stat	p-value
26	238	-0.36%	-1.27	0.21	262	-0.20%	-0.74	0.46	268	-0.63%	-3.94	0.00
27	237	-0.11%	-0.33	0.74	260	-0.18%	-0.85	0.39	267	-0.59%	-3.44	0.00
28	237	-0.02%	-0.04	0.97	258	-0.08%	-0.37	0.71	266	-0.27%	-1.83	0.07
29	235	-0.16%	-0.35	0.72	257	-0.26%	-0.80	0.42	265	-0.31%	-2.10	0.04
30	234	-0.34%	-0.97	0.33	256	-0.26%	-0.74	0.46	264	-0.34%	-1.61	0.11
31	232	-0.50%	-1.40	0.16	256	-0.22%	-0.77	0.44	263	-0.30%	-1.39	0.16
32	230	-0.05%	-0.15	0.88	254	-0.19%	-0.73	0.46	262	-0.16%	-0.75	0.46
33	226	-0.28%	-0.82	0.41	251	0.17%	0.64	0.52	261	-0.12%	-0.57	0.57
34	225	-0.04%	-0.13	0.90	251	-0.40%	-1.76	0.08	259	-0.06%	-0.28	0.78
35	223	0.34%	0.94	0.35	250	0.03%	0.11	0.91	259	0.13%	0.56	0.57
36	222	0.34%	1.10	0.27	248	0.28%	0.93	0.35	258	0.14%	0.57	0.57
37	219	0.43%	1.13	0.26	245	0.01%	0.06	0.95	257	0.17%	0.71	0.48
38	218	0.21%	0.56	0.58	244	0.02%	0.06	0.95	256	0.17%	0.73	0.47
39	216	0.65%	1.50	0.13	243	0.02%	0.08	0.94	254	-0.09%	-0.54	0.59
40	215	0.19%	0.42	0.68	241	0.27%	0.89	0.38	254	-0.15%	-0.90	0.37
41	213	0.15%	0.40	0.69	240	0.24%	0.77	0.44	253	-0.05%	-0.21	0.84
42	210	0.50%	1.00	0.32	239	0.20%	0.54	0.59	252	0.04%	0.15	0.88
43	209	-0.05%	-0.11	0.91	238	-0.21%	-0.81	0.42	250	0.07%	0.25	0.80
44	207	0.58%	1.55	0.12	237	0.34%	0.95	0.34	248	0.06%	0.23	0.82
45	205	0.47%	1.33	0.18	236	-0.03%	-0.12	0.90	247	-0.11%	-0.50	0.62
46	204	-0.28%	-0.85	0.40	233	-0.06%	-0.20	0.84	245	-0.16%	-0.75	0.45
47	203	0.03%	0.09	0.93	232	0.19%	0.62	0.53	244	-0.05%	-0.23	0.82
48	201	0.22%	0.78	0.44	232	0.18%	0.64	0.52	243	-0.09%	-0.45	0.65
49	199	0.51%	1.40	0.16	230	0.09%	0.40	0.69	242	-0.19%	-0.96	0.34
50	197	-0.55%	-1.64	0.10	228	-0.23%	-0.85	0.40	241	0.00%	-0.02	0.98

End	3-months window				6-months window				12-months window			
month	# Obs.	Abnormal Return	t-stat	p-value	# Obs.	Abnormal Return	t-stat	p-value	# Obs.	Abnormal Return	t-stat	p-value
51	190	-0.51%	-1.21	0.23	226	-0.21%	-0.71	0.48	240	0.04%	0.17	0.86
52	186	0.13%	0.30	0.76	225	0.03%	0.09	0.93	239	0.05%	0.20	0.84
53	182	0.28%	0.70	0.48	223	0.02%	0.05	0.96	238	0.12%	0.55	0.58
54	180	0.63%	1.48	0.14	222	0.25%	0.76	0.45	237	0.04%	0.19	0.85
55	179	0.25%	0.59	0.56	221	0.16%	0.50	0.62	236	0.16%	0.70	0.48
56	178	0.03%	0.08	0.94	220	0.23%	0.73	0.46	235	0.09%	0.39	0.70
57	178	-0.09%	-0.29	0.77	219	0.28%	0.89	0.37	234	0.09%	0.36	0.72
58	177	0.06%	0.17	0.86	218	0.32%	1.03	0.30	233	0.13%	0.49	0.62
59	175	0.56%	1.42	0.15	217	0.37%	1.25	0.21	232	0.26%	0.98	0.33
60	173	1.55%	3.36	0.00	216	0.47%	1.46	0.15	231	0.32%	1.14	0.25
61	170	1.22%	2.68	0.01	215	0.55%	1.66	0.10	230	0.27%	1.01	0.31
62	169	0.66%	1.86	0.06	214	0.65%	2.15	0.03	229	0.29%	1.07	0.28
63	168	-0.05%	-0.14	0.89	212	0.54%	1.77	0.08	228	0.29%	1.05	0.29
64	167	-0.45%	-1.17	0.24	211	0.60%	1.92	0.05	227	0.35%	1.23	0.22
65	167	0.01%	0.01	0.99	210	0.36%	1.12	0.26	226	0.24%	0.89	0.38
66	166	0.96%	2.54	0.01	209	0.14%	0.45	0.65	225	0.15%	0.59	0.56
67	164	0.47%	1.15	0.25	208	0.26%	0.89	0.37	224	0.32%	1.43	0.15
68	163	1.33%	3.01	0.00	207	0.52%	1.52	0.13	223	0.43%	1.78	0.07
69	162	0.73%	1.84	0.07	206	0.54%	1.60	0.11	222	0.50%	2.04	0.04
70	160	0.81%	1.94	0.05	205	0.52%	1.85	0.06	221	0.44%	1.98	0.05
71	159	0.72%	1.42	0.15	202	0.67%	2.32	0.02	220	0.39%	1.64	0.10
72	158	0.38%	0.87	0.38	201	0.65%	2.02	0.04	219	0.33%	1.40	0.16

Table A.2: Abnormal Portfolio Returns for Rolling Short Investment Horizons (4-factor)

This table presents the 4-factor abnormal returns of equal-weighted portfolios. The column labeled '# Obs.' contains the number of monthly portfolios in the sample. 'T-stat' shows the test statistic associated with the abnormal return estimates, and 'p-value' is the corresponding (degrees-of-freedom-adjusted) probability value of the estimate being different from zero. Panel A contains the data for Figure 2, Panel B for Figure A.2.

Panel A: 4-factor model intercepts (OLS)

	3-months window				6-months window				12-months window			
End month	# Obs.	Abnormal Return	t-stat	p-value	# Obs.	Abnormal Return	t-stat	p-value	# Obs.	Abnormal Return	t-stat	p-value
3	261	0.57%	1.87	0.06								
4	261	0.16%	0.59	0.55								
5	261	-0.28%	-1.22	0.22								
6	261	-0.65%	-2.75	0.01	275	0.04%	0.17	0.87				
7	261	-0.62%	-2.35	0.02	275	-0.24%	-1.12	0.26				
8	260	-0.64%	-2.58	0.01	275	-0.36%	-1.77	0.08				
9	260	-0.83%	-3.20	0.00	275	-0.67%	-3.19	0.00				
10	260	-1.13%	-4.25	0.00	275	-0.90%	-4.02	0.00				
11	260	-1.25%	-4.75	0.00	275	-0.97%	-4.32	0.00				
12	260	-1.57%	-5.63	0.00	275	-1.12%	-4.82	0.00	281	-0.41%	-2.11	0.04
13	257	-1.41%	-4.72	0.00	275	-1.23%	-5.38	0.00	281	-0.60%	-3.11	0.00
14	253	-1.60%	-5.86	0.00	274	-1.45%	-6.16	0.00	280	-0.81%	-4.21	0.00
15	252	-1.56%	-5.73	0.00	273	-1.52%	-6.17	0.00	279	-0.94%	-4.86	0.00
16	250	-1.57%	-5.48	0.00	272	-1.58%	-6.16	0.00	278	-1.13%	-5.59	0.00
17	250	-1.41%	-4.73	0.00	271	-1.66%	-6.54	0.00	277	-1.22%	-5.97	0.00
18	249	-1.04%	-3.54	0.00	270	-1.49%	-5.94	0.00	276	-1.24%	-5.87	0.00

End month	3-months window # Obs.	Abnormal Return	t-stat	p-value	6-months window # Obs.	Abnormal Return	t-stat	p-value	12-months window # Obs.	Abnormal Return	t-stat	p-value
19	248	-0.92%	-3.12	0.00	269	-1.36%	-5.57	0.00	275	-1.32%	-6.17	0.00
20	246	-0.87%	-2.86	0.00	268	-1.29%	-5.12	0.00	274	-1.39%	-6.38	0.00
21	244	-1.04%	-3.20	0.00	267	-1.12%	-4.30	0.00	273	-1.35%	-5.99	0.00
22	241	-0.72%	-2.33	0.02	266	-1.01%	-3.98	0.00	272	-1.32%	-5.89	0.00
23	240	-0.81%	-2.78	0.01	265	-0.82%	-3.19	0.00	271	-1.30%	-5.83	0.00
24	240	-1.01%	-3.43	0.00	264	-0.95%	-3.66	0.00	270	-1.20%	-5.42	0.00
25	239	-0.69%	-2.34	0.02	263	-0.90%	-3.57	0.00	269	-1.11%	-5.04	0.00
26	238	-0.68%	-2.31	0.02	262	-0.87%	-3.65	0.00	268	-1.07%	-4.88	0.00
27	237	-0.27%	-0.91	0.36	260	-0.69%	-3.00	0.00	267	-0.85%	-3.96	0.00
28	237	-0.37%	-1.21	0.23	258	-0.60%	-2.51	0.01	266	-0.78%	-3.63	0.00
29	235	-0.41%	-1.22	0.22	257	-0.51%	-2.05	0.04	265	-0.67%	-3.09	0.00
30	234	-0.58%	-1.76	0.08	256	-0.44%	-1.71	0.09	264	-0.72%	-3.27	0.00
31	232	-0.73%	-2.19	0.03	256	-0.60%	-2.31	0.02	263	-0.73%	-3.34	0.00
32	230	-0.45%	-1.41	0.16	254	-0.37%	-1.28	0.20	262	-0.61%	-2.81	0.01
33	226	-0.19%	-0.60	0.55	251	-0.31%	-1.06	0.29	261	-0.54%	-2.47	0.01
34	225	0.12%	0.35	0.73	251	-0.17%	-0.54	0.59	259	-0.43%	-1.89	0.06
35	223	0.07%	0.20	0.84	250	-0.21%	-0.75	0.45	259	-0.35%	-1.51	0.13
36	222	0.14%	0.45	0.66	248	0.06%	0.22	0.82	258	-0.19%	-0.79	0.43
37	219	0.40%	1.24	0.21	245	0.27%	0.97	0.33	257	-0.18%	-0.73	0.46
38	218	0.24%	0.75	0.45	244	0.09%	0.34	0.73	256	-0.13%	-0.52	0.60
39	216	0.35%	0.98	0.33	243	0.11%	0.44	0.66	254	-0.03%	-0.12	0.90
40	215	0.12%	0.37	0.71	241	0.15%	0.58	0.56	254	0.03%	0.12	0.90
41	213	0.13%	0.38	0.71	240	0.12%	0.48	0.64	253	-0.16%	-0.72	0.47
42	210	0.20%	0.60	0.55	239	0.03%	0.11	0.91	252	-0.08%	-0.36	0.72
43	209	-0.10%	-0.30	0.76	238	-0.05%	-0.21	0.83	250	0.00%	0.00	1.00
44	207	0.40%	1.23	0.22	237	0.18%	0.71	0.48	248	0.03%	0.12	0.90
45	205	0.13%	0.42	0.68	236	0.07%	0.29	0.77	247	-0.02%	-0.08	0.93

End month	3-months window # Obs.	Abnormal Return	t-stat	p-value	6-months window # Obs.	Abnormal Return	t-stat	p-value	12-months window # Obs.	Abnormal Return	t-stat	p-value
46	204	-0.28%	-0.98	0.33	233	-0.11%	-0.48	0.63	245	-0.09%	-0.47	0.64
47	203	-0.41%	-1.54	0.13	232	0.06%	0.26	0.80	244	-0.05%	-0.27	0.79
48	201	-0.30%	-1.06	0.29	232	-0.08%	-0.35	0.72	243	-0.09%	-0.46	0.65
49	199	0.23%	0.72	0.47	230	-0.20%	-0.90	0.37	242	-0.12%	-0.63	0.53
50	197	-0.30%	-0.84	0.40	228	-0.33%	-1.48	0.14	241	-0.10%	-0.55	0.58
51	190	-0.16%	-0.45	0.65	226	-0.25%	-1.06	0.29	240	-0.09%	-0.50	0.62
52	186	-0.26%	-0.80	0.42	225	-0.03%	-0.11	0.91	239	-0.11%	-0.59	0.56
53	182	-0.05%	-0.15	0.88	223	-0.20%	-0.85	0.40	238	-0.05%	-0.26	0.80
54	180	0.20%	0.62	0.54	222	-0.03%	-0.13	0.90	237	-0.05%	-0.31	0.76
55	179	0.02%	0.08	0.93	221	-0.16%	-0.69	0.49	236	-0.11%	-0.64	0.52
56	178	-0.22%	-0.69	0.49	220	-0.12%	-0.52	0.61	235	-0.19%	-1.08	0.28
57	178	-0.48%	-1.71	0.09	219	-0.14%	-0.63	0.53	234	-0.18%	-1.00	0.32
58	177	-0.26%	-0.85	0.40	218	-0.04%	-0.19	0.85	233	-0.10%	-0.54	0.59
59	175	0.32%	0.83	0.41	217	-0.09%	-0.38	0.71	232	-0.10%	-0.55	0.58
60	173	0.97%	2.30	0.02	216	-0.02%	-0.09	0.93	231	-0.03%	-0.16	0.87
61	170	0.97%	2.42	0.02	215	0.14%	0.49	0.62	230	-0.08%	-0.39	0.70
62	169	0.35%	1.04	0.30	214	0.17%	0.67	0.50	229	-0.02%	-0.08	0.94
63	168	-0.40%	-1.24	0.22	212	0.21%	0.73	0.46	228	-0.09%	-0.43	0.67
64	167	-0.73%	-1.99	0.05	211	0.12%	0.43	0.67	227	-0.12%	-0.57	0.57
65	167	-0.68%	-1.51	0.13	210	-0.08%	-0.29	0.77	226	-0.23%	-1.13	0.26
66	166	-0.18%	-0.40	0.69	209	-0.22%	-0.80	0.42	225	-0.20%	-0.99	0.33
67	164	0.12%	0.30	0.77	208	-0.17%	-0.60	0.55	224	-0.06%	-0.31	0.75
68	163	0.75%	2.16	0.03	207	0.08%	0.26	0.79	223	0.05%	0.23	0.82
69	162	0.35%	1.06	0.29	206	0.20%	0.70	0.48	222	0.13%	0.59	0.56
70	160	0.54%	1.36	0.18	205	0.24%	0.93	0.35	221	0.11%	0.48	0.63
71	159	0.20%	0.49	0.63	202	0.33%	1.33	0.18	220	0.04%	0.17	0.86
72	158	-0.07%	-0.17	0.86	201	0.24%	0.96	0.34	219	-0.11%	-0.52	0.60

Panel B: 4-factor model intercepts (GARCH (1,1))

End month	3-months window # Obs.	Abnormal Return	t-stat	p-value	6-months window # Obs.	Abnormal Return	t-stat	p-value	12-months window # Obs.	Abnormal Return	t-stat	p-value
3	261	0.74%	3.27	0.00								
4	261	0.27%	1.19	0.23								
5	261	-0.17%	-0.81	0.42								
6	261	-0.47%	-2.46	0.01	275	0.10%	0.62	0.54				
7	261	-0.53%	-2.20	0.03	275	-0.17%	-0.97	0.33				
8	260	-0.60%	-2.68	0.01	275	-0.31%	-1.80	0.07				
9	260	-0.90%	-4.79	0.00	275	-0.60%	-3.74	0.00				
10	260	-0.93%	-4.36	0.00	275	-0.75%	-4.24	0.00				
11	260	-1.00%	-4.53	0.00	275	-0.79%	-4.37	0.00				
12	260	-1.21%	-5.74	0.00	275	-0.99%	-6.66	0.00	281	-0.26%	-1.89	0.06
13	257	-1.14%	-5.95	0.00	275	-0.87%	-5.34	0.00	281	-0.48%	-3.53	0.00
14	253	-1.41%	-6.64	0.00	274	-1.13%	-7.01	0.00	280	-0.68%	-5.11	0.00
15	252	-1.52%	-7.88	0.00	273	-1.21%	-6.59	0.00	279	-0.82%	-6.33	0.00
16	250	-1.35%	-5.22	0.00	272	-1.18%	-5.90	0.00	278	-0.98%	-7.85	0.00
17	250	-1.02%	-4.30	0.00	271	-1.33%	-6.27	0.00	277	-1.03%	-7.47	0.00
18	249	-0.77%	-3.65	0.00	270	-1.08%	-5.89	0.00	276	-1.06%	-8.11	0.00
19	248	-0.82%	-4.03	0.00	269	-1.19%	-6.68	0.00	275	-1.12%	-8.81	0.00
20	246	-0.84%	-2.94	0.00	268	-1.08%	-6.21	0.00	274	-1.14%	-8.32	0.00
21	244	-0.50%	-1.92	0.05	267	-0.73%	-4.29	0.00	273	-1.31%	-9.63	0.00
22	241	-0.99%	-3.26	0.00	266	-0.79%	-3.63	0.00	272	-1.14%	-8.26	0.00
23	240	-0.71%	-2.52	0.01	265	-0.81%	-3.75	0.00	271	-1.05%	-6.60	0.00
24	240	-0.81%	-3.13	0.00	264	-0.66%	-3.06	0.00	270	-0.94%	-6.28	0.00
25	239	-0.52%	-1.94	0.05	263	-0.47%	-2.27	0.02	269	-0.83%	-5.38	0.00

End month	3-months window				6-months window				12-months window			
	# Obs.	Abnormal Return	t-stat	p-value	# Obs.	Abnormal Return	t-stat	p-value	# Obs.	Abnormal Return	t-stat	p-value
26	238	-0.55%	-2.12	0.03	262	-0.62%	-2.58	0.01	268	-0.77%	-4.54	0.00
27	237	-0.46%	-1.69	0.09	260	-0.53%	-2.57	0.01	267	-0.65%	-3.74	0.00
28	237	-0.39%	-1.06	0.29	258	-0.39%	-2.02	0.04	266	-0.55%	-3.39	0.00
29	235	-0.41%	-1.00	0.32	257	-0.49%	-1.68	0.09	265	-0.47%	-2.80	0.01
30	234	-0.58%	-1.46	0.14	256	-0.43%	-1.34	0.18	264	-0.56%	-3.08	0.00
31	232	-0.73%	-1.97	0.05	256	-0.56%	-2.15	0.03	263	-0.52%	-2.88	0.00
32	230	-0.35%	-1.46	0.15	254	-0.50%	-2.31	0.02	262	-0.46%	-2.62	0.01
33	226	-0.19%	-0.54	0.59	251	-0.25%	-1.19	0.23	261	-0.48%	-2.69	0.01
34	225	0.07%	0.20	0.84	251	-0.14%	-0.65	0.52	259	-0.46%	-2.55	0.01
35	223	0.07%	0.18	0.86	250	-0.31%	-1.48	0.14	259	-0.37%	-1.83	0.07
36	222	0.08%	0.29	0.77	248	-0.04%	-0.17	0.86	258	-0.18%	-0.94	0.35
37	219	0.40%	1.04	0.30	245	-0.21%	-1.18	0.24	257	-0.18%	-0.56	0.57
38	218	0.04%	0.13	0.90	244	-0.17%	-0.68	0.50	256	-0.14%	-0.66	0.51
39	216	0.34%	0.73	0.46	243	0.11%	0.34	0.73	254	0.02%	0.15	0.88
40	215	-0.04%	-0.09	0.93	241	0.15%	0.47	0.64	254	0.01%	0.05	0.96
41	213	0.13%	0.32	0.75	240	0.00%	-0.01	1.00	253	-0.32%	-1.65	0.10
42	210	0.20%	0.52	0.60	239	-0.03%	-0.09	0.93	252	-0.22%	-1.22	0.22
43	209	0.06%	0.18	0.86	238	-0.06%	-0.19	0.85	250	-0.16%	-0.82	0.41
44	207	0.31%	0.99	0.32	237	0.18%	0.60	0.55	248	-0.10%	-0.51	0.61
45	205	0.05%	0.17	0.87	236	-0.08%	-0.40	0.69	247	-0.09%	-0.50	0.62
46	204	-0.42%	-1.54	0.12	233	-0.23%	-1.08	0.28	245	-0.10%	-0.67	0.50
47	203	-0.33%	-1.36	0.17	232	-0.09%	-0.38	0.70	244	-0.12%	-0.74	0.46
48	201	-0.24%	-0.80	0.42	232	-0.12%	-0.54	0.59	243	-0.16%	-0.96	0.34
49	199	0.24%	0.68	0.50	230	-0.19%	-0.75	0.45	242	-0.20%	-1.11	0.27
50	197	-0.19%	-0.57	0.57	228	-0.32%	-1.25	0.21	241	-0.22%	-1.15	0.25

End month	3-months window				6-months window				12-months window			
	# Obs.	Abnormal Return	t-stat	p-value	# Obs.	Abnormal Return	t-stat	p-value	# Obs.	Abnormal Return	t-stat	p-value
51	190	-0.04%	-0.10	0.92	226	-0.22%	-0.84	0.40	240	-0.22%	-1.18	0.24
52	186	-0.26%	-0.66	0.51	225	-0.03%	-0.09	0.92	239	-0.13%	-0.62	0.53
53	182	-0.15%	-0.46	0.64	223	-0.19%	-0.71	0.48	238	-0.04%	-0.19	0.85
54	180	0.20%	0.56	0.58	222	-0.03%	-0.11	0.91	237	-0.13%	-0.68	0.49
55	179	0.02%	0.08	0.94	221	-0.26%	-1.04	0.30	236	-0.13%	-0.65	0.52
56	178	-0.27%	-0.77	0.44	220	-0.12%	-0.48	0.63	235	-0.19%	-0.97	0.33
57	178	-0.38%	-1.21	0.23	219	-0.15%	-0.57	0.57	234	-0.18%	-0.88	0.38
58	177	-0.21%	-0.69	0.49	218	-0.06%	-0.26	0.79	233	-0.10%	-0.47	0.64
59	175	0.32%	0.71	0.48	217	-0.09%	-0.34	0.73	232	-0.10%	-0.49	0.63
60	173	1.09%	2.76	0.01	216	-0.02%	-0.08	0.93	231	-0.03%	-0.14	0.89
61	170	1.19%	2.92	0.00	215	0.14%	0.44	0.66	230	-0.08%	-0.33	0.74
62	169	0.57%	1.83	0.07	214	0.29%	0.97	0.33	229	-0.01%	-0.07	0.94
63	168	-0.45%	-1.41	0.16	212	0.37%	1.30	0.19	228	-0.05%	-0.24	0.81
64	167	-0.73%	-1.68	0.09	211	0.32%	1.09	0.27	227	-0.07%	-0.35	0.73
65	167	-0.68%	-1.24	0.22	210	-0.08%	-0.27	0.79	226	-0.17%	-0.83	0.40
66	166	-0.18%	-0.33	0.74	209	-0.22%	-0.75	0.45	225	-0.11%	-0.58	0.56
67	164	0.23%	0.49	0.63	208	-0.17%	-0.56	0.57	224	0.20%	1.07	0.28
68	163	0.79%	1.96	0.05	207	0.08%	0.23	0.82	223	0.37%	1.75	0.08
69	162	0.35%	1.01	0.31	206	0.22%	0.62	0.53	222	0.23%	1.07	0.29
70	160	0.53%	1.16	0.25	205	0.21%	0.89	0.37	221	0.28%	1.21	0.23
71	159	0.20%	0.44	0.66	202	0.30%	1.21	0.23	220	0.04%	0.17	0.87
72	158	-0.06%	-0.15	0.88	201	0.24%	0.85	0.40	219	-0.11%	-0.49	0.62

Table A.3: Abnormal Return for Value-Weighted Deviation Quartile Portfolios (GARCH)

This table presents the results for the heteroscedasticity-controlled GARCH (1,1) specification of the asset pricing model. For a description of the table content, refer to Table 10, Section 5.4.1, Page 72.

Panel A: 3-Factor Abnormal Returns

	1 Year (281 months)		2 Years (282 months)		3 Years (282 months)	
Deviation Quartile	Abnormal Return	t-stat	Abnormal Return	t-stat	Abnormal Return	t-stat
Lowest	0.94%	3.24	0.71%	3.41	0.48%	2.61
Q2	0.34%	1.54	-0.01%	-0.09	0.06%	0.42
Q3	-0.03%	-0.13	-0.10%	-0.50	-0.09%	-0.49
Highest	-0.61%	-1.88	-0.63%	-2.50	-0.49%	-2.06
High - Low	-1.68%	-3.93	-1.30%	-4.39	-1.11%	-3.60

Panel B: 4-Factor Abnormal Returns

	1 Year (281 months)		2 Years (282 months)		3 Years (282 months)	
Deviation Quartile	Abnormal Return	t-stat	Abnormal Return	t-stat	Abnormal Return	t-stat
Lowest	0.95%	3.34	0.72%	3.51	0.50%	2.76
Q2	0.35%	1.57	-0.01%	-0.08	0.07%	0.45
Q3	-0.01%	-0.04	-0.23%	-1.13	-0.07%	-0.40
Highest	-0.72%	-2.42	-0.75%	-3.12	-0.64%	-3.10
High - Low	-1.70%	-4.43	-1.39%	-4.67	-1.12%	-3.72

Table A.4: Abnormal Return for Equal-Weighted Deviation Quartile Portfolios (GARCH)

This table presents the results for the heteroscedasticity-controlled GARCH (1,1) specification of the asset pricing model. For a description of the table content, refer to Table 11, Section 5.4.1, in the main text.

Panel A: 3-Factor Abnormal Returns

	1 Year (281 months)		2 Years (282 months)		3 Years (282 months)	
Deviation Quartile	Abnormal Return	t-stat	Abnormal Return	t-stat	Abnormal Return	t-stat
Lowest	0.27%	1.29	-0.12%	-0.63	0.12%	0.65
Q2	0.12%	0.72	-0.31%	-2.09	-0.20%	-1.49
Q3	-0.27%	-1.56	-0.61%	-4.08	-0.55%	-3.52
Highest	-0.72%	-2.34	-0.88%	-3.59	-0.54%	-2.14
High - Low	-1.11%	-3.16	-0.80%	-3.42	-0.65%	-3.03

Panel B: 4-Factor Abnormal Returns

	1 Year (281 months)		2 Years (282 months)		3 Years (282 months)	
Deviation Quartile	Abnormal Return	t-stat	Abnormal Return	t-stat	Abnormal Return	t-stat
Lowest	0.35%	1.67	-0.17%	-0.95	0.03%	0.17
Q2	0.12%	0.68	-0.30%	-1.95	-0.25%	-1.95
Q3	-0.43%	-2.59	-0.65%	-3.66	-0.56%	-3.35
Highest	-1.26%	-4.55	-1.17%	-5.85	-0.93%	-4.53
High - Low	-1.63%	-4.96	-1.01%	-5.28	-0.86%	-4.15

Table A.5: Abnormal Value-Weighted Portfolio Returns per Deviation and Size Quartiles (GARCH)

This table presents the results for the heteroscedasticity-controlled GARCH (1,1) specification of the asset pricing model. For a description of the table content, refer to Table 13, Section 5.4.1, in the main text.

Panel A: 3-factor abnormal returns

'1 Year' portfolio time-series (236 months)

	Big		Q2		Q3		Small		Small - Big	
Deviation Quartile	Abnormal Return	t-stat	Abnormal Return	t-stat	Abnormal Return	t-stat	Abnormal Return	t-stat	Abnormal Return	t-stat
Lowest	0.96%	2.58	0.51%	1.43	0.10%	0.24	-1.31%	-3.16	-2.16%	-3.47
Q2	0.46%	1.71	0.59%	2.30	-0.09%	-0.23	-0.20%	-0.48	-1.44%	-2.58
Q3	-0.25%	-0.98	-0.19%	-0.59	-0.07%	-0.20	-0.75%	-1.57	-1.25%	-2.25
Highest	-1.09%	-2.15	-0.85%	-2.10	-0.56%	-1.49	-1.92%	-3.62	-1.24%	-1.85
High - Low	-2.35%	-3.52	-1.04%	-2.13	-0.98%	-2.01	-0.66%	-1.05		

'2 Year' portfolio time-series (270 months)

Deviation Quartile	Big Abnormal Return	Big t-stat	Q2 Abnormal Return	Q2 t-stat	Q3 Abnormal Return	Q3 t-stat	Small Abnormal Return	Small t-stat	Small - Big Abnormal Return	Small - Big t-stat
Lowest	0.87%	3.35	0.09%	0.39	-0.20%	-0.79	-1.32%	-3.47	-2.59%	-4.39
Q2	0.15%	0.81	0.06%	0.28	-0.68%	-2.65	-1.21%	-2.81	-1.60%	-3.49
Q3	-0.18%	-0.73	-0.67%	-2.84	-0.69%	-2.26	-1.15%	-2.72	-0.99%	-2.09
Highest	-0.62%	-1.71	-0.72%	-2.77	-1.14%	-4.06	-1.68%	-4.36	-0.79%	-1.62
High - Low	-1.43%	-3.44	-0.54%	-1.87	-0.82%	-2.26	-0.12%	-0.30		

'3 Year' portfolio time-series (274 months)

Deviation Quartile	Big Abnormal Return	Big t-stat	Q2 Abnormal Return	Q2 t-stat	Q3 Abnormal Return	Q3 t-stat	Small Abnormal Return	Small t-stat	Small - Big Abnormal Return	Small - Big t-stat
Lowest	0.58%	2.44	0.20%	1.01	-0.34%	-1.29	-0.77%	-2.17	-1.53%	-3.31
Q2	0.23%	1.39	-0.19%	-0.88	-0.63%	-2.81	-0.88%	-1.96	-1.33%	-3.05
Q3	-0.03%	-0.13	-0.30%	-1.39	-0.46%	-1.61	-0.91%	-2.38	-0.97%	-2.12
Highest	-0.50%	-1.68	-0.69%	-2.78	-0.96%	-3.48	-1.25%	-3.39	-0.80%	-1.68
High - Low	-1.20%	-2.88	-0.79%	-2.73	-0.62%	-2.01	-0.34%	-0.69		

Panel B: 4-factor abnormal returns

'1 Year' portfolio time-series (236 months)

	Big		Q2		Q3		Small		Small - Big	
Deviation Quartile	Abnormal Return	t-stat	Abnormal Return	t-stat	Abnormal Return	t-stat	Abnormal Return	t-stat	Abnormal Return	t-stat
Lowest	0.97%	2.67	0.55%	1.35	0.13%	0.34	-1.33%	-3.21	-2.26%	-3.63
Q2	0.45%	1.65	0.56%	2.11	0.04%	0.11	-0.52%	-1.46	-1.27%	-2.42
Q3	-0.21%	-0.81	-0.21%	-0.66	-0.18%	-0.48	-1.09%	-2.15	-1.37%	-2.17
Highest	-0.47%	-0.99	-1.02%	-2.59	-0.63%	-1.63	-2.76%	-5.71	-1.50%	-2.13
High - Low	-1.36%	-2.39	-1.34%	-2.79	-1.12%	-2.23	-1.39%	-2.41		

'2 Year' portfolio time-series (270 months)

	Big		Q2		Q3		Small		Small - Big	
Deviation Quartile	Abnormal Return	t-stat	Abnormal Return	t-stat	Abnormal Return	t-stat	Abnormal Return	t-stat	Abnormal Return	t-stat
Lowest	0.89%	3.49	0.10%	0.43	-0.24%	-0.90	-1.84%	-5.36	-2.49%	-5.11
Q2	0.13%	0.72	0.02%	0.08	-0.77%	-2.84	-1.38%	-3.67	-1.73%	-4.38
Q3	-0.17%	-0.71	-0.70%	-2.72	-0.54%	-2.16	-0.97%	-2.26	-0.92%	-1.93
Highest	-0.69%	-1.96	-0.83%	-3.23	-1.04%	-3.73	-1.97%	-6.16	-1.06%	-2.18
High - Low	-1.45%	-3.55	-0.75%	-2.70	-0.98%	-2.87	-0.49%	-1.25		

'3 Year' portfolio time-series (274 months)

	Big		Q2		Q3		Small		Small - Big	
Deviation Quartile	Abnormal Return	t-stat	Abnormal Return	t-stat	Abnormal Return	t-stat	Abnormal Return	t-stat	Abnormal Return	t-stat
Lowest	0.59%	2.54	0.21%	1.06	-0.39%	-1.50	-1.25%	-3.79	-1.81%	-4.34
Q2	0.23%	1.39	-0.27%	-1.31	-0.69%	-3.20	-1.15%	-3.39	-1.53%	-4.28
Q3	0.00%	-0.02	-0.35%	-1.61	-0.64%	-2.53	-1.21%	-3.63	-1.18%	-2.63
Highest	-0.58%	-2.01	-0.90%	-3.91	-0.97%	-4.36	-1.45%	-2.52	-1.02%	-2.24
High - Low	-1.10%	-2.68	-0.96%	-3.14	-0.75%	-2.67	-0.50%	-1.09		

Table A.6: Abnormal Equal-Weighted Portfolio Returns per Deviation and Size Quartiles (OLS)

This table presents the results for the equal-weighted portfolio returns. For a description of the table content, refer to Table 13, Section 5.4.2, in the main text.

Panel A: 3-factor abnormal returns

'1 Year' portfolio time-series (236 months)

	Big		Q2		Q3		Small		Small - Big	
Deviation Quartile	Abnormal Return	t-stat	Abnormal Return	t-stat	Abnormal Return	t-stat	Abnormal Return	t-stat	Abnormal Return	t-stat
Lowest	0.84%	2.37	0.55%	1.50	0.42%	0.95	-1.23%	-2.32	-2.06%	-3.41
Q2	0.68%	2.23	0.41%	1.09	-0.03%	-0.09	-1.05%	-2.30	-1.73%	-3.16
Q3	-0.55%	-1.51	-0.34%	-0.94	-0.53%	-1.27	-1.23%	-2.39	-0.68%	-1.17
Highest	-0.94%	-1.91	-1.22%	-2.62	-1.24%	-2.46	-2.08%	-3.33	-1.14%	-1.65
High - Low	-1.78%	-3.05	-1.76%	-3.03	-1.66%	-2.65	-0.86%	-1.10		

'2 Year' portfolio time-series (270 months)

	Big		Q2		Q3		Small		Small - Big	
Deviation Quartile	Abnormal Return	t-stat	Abnormal Return	t-stat	Abnormal Return	t-stat	Abnormal Return	t-stat	Abnormal Return	t-stat
Lowest	0.79%	3.06	0.13%	0.51	-0.43%	-1.44	-0.81%	-1.65	-1.60%	-2.76
Q2	0.18%	0.75	-0.17%	-0.64	-0.86%	-2.54	-1.15%	-2.59	-1.33%	-2.60
Q3	-0.52%	-1.98	-0.72%	-2.61	-0.85%	-2.44	-0.68%	-1.19	-0.15%	-0.25
Highest	-0.89%	-2.29	-1.13%	-3.01	-1.30%	-2.99	-1.25%	-2.11	-0.35%	-0.58
High - Low	-1.69%	-3.68	-1.26%	-3.10	-0.87%	-1.86	-0.44%	-0.81		

'3 Year' portfolio time-series (274 months)

	Big		Q2		Q3		Small		Small - Big	
Deviation Quartile	Abnormal Return	t-stat	Abnormal Return	t-stat	Abnormal Return	t-stat	Abnormal Return	t-stat	Abnormal Return	t-stat
Lowest	0.55%	2.47	0.19%	0.78	-0.28%	-0.88	0.15%	0.28	-0.40%	-0.66
Q2	0.19%	0.97	-0.33%	-1.54	-0.94%	-2.98	-0.48%	-1.14	-0.66%	-1.45
Q3	-0.41%	-1.74	-0.74%	-2.80	-0.72%	-2.30	-0.17%	-0.31	0.24%	0.42
Highest	-0.70%	-2.19	-0.95%	-2.83	-1.23%	-2.83	-0.26%	-0.42	0.44%	0.74
High - Low	-1.26%	-3.22	-1.15%	-3.05	-0.95%	-2.55	-0.41%	-0.75		

Panel B: 4-factor abnormal returns

'1 Year' portfolio time-series (236 months)

	Big		Q2		Q3		Small		Small - Big	
Deviation Quartile	Abnormal Return	t-stat	Abnormal Return	t-stat	Abnormal Return	t-stat	Abnormal Return	t-stat	Abnormal Return	t-stat
Lowest	0.97%	2.85	0.65%	1.80	0.46%	1.04	-1.25%	-2.35	-2.23%	-3.73
Q2	0.70%	2.28	0.44%	1.16	-0.08%	-0.22	-1.23%	-2.82	-1.94%	-3.65
Q3	-0.66%	-1.83	-0.45%	-1.30	-0.73%	-1.85	-1.60%	-3.54	-0.94%	-1.68
Highest	-1.11%	-2.29	-1.46%	-3.34	-1.56%	-3.42	-2.62%	-5.14	-1.51%	-2.34
High - Low	-2.08%	-3.81	-2.11%	-3.95	-2.02%	-3.49	-1.36%	-1.93		

'2 Year' portfolio time-series (270 months)

	Big		Q2		Q3		Small		Small - Big	
Deviation Quartile	Abnormal Return	t-stat	Abnormal Return	t-stat	Abnormal Return	t-stat	Abnormal Return	t-stat	Abnormal Return	t-stat
Lowest	0.90%	3.56	0.16%	0.60	-0.47%	-1.58	-1.11%	-2.49	-2.00%	-3.91
Q2	0.23%	0.93	-0.21%	-0.79	-1.00%	-3.08	-1.45%	-3.64	-1.68%	-3.64
Q3	-0.58%	-2.22	-0.84%	-3.16	-1.09%	-3.49	-1.11%	-2.28	-0.53%	-0.93
Highest	-1.06%	-2.82	-1.33%	-3.82	-1.66%	-4.59	-1.82%	-4.11	-0.77%	-1.41
High - Low	-1.95%	-4.63	-1.49%	-3.94	-1.18%	-2.85	-0.72%	-1.39		

'3 Year' portfolio time-series (274 months)

	Big		Q2		Q3		Small		Small - Big	
Deviation Quartile	Abnormal Return	t-stat	Abnormal Return	t-stat	Abnormal Return	t-stat	Abnormal Return	t-stat	Abnormal Return	t-stat
Lowest	0.61%	2.77	0.18%	0.73	-0.40%	-1.31	-0.22%	-0.47	-0.83%	-1.56
Q2	0.20%	1.04	-0.38%	-1.79	-1.13%	-3.86	-0.78%	-2.16	-0.98%	-2.47
Q3	-0.46%	-1.98	-0.88%	-3.55	-0.93%	-3.39	-0.62%	-1.42	-0.16%	-0.32
Highest	-0.86%	-2.82	-1.17%	-3.91	-1.58%	-4.37	-0.83%	-1.74	0.03%	0.05
High - Low	-1.47%	-4.06	-1.36%	-3.90	-1.18%	-3.48	-0.61%	-1.15		

Table A.7: Abnormal Equal-Weighted Portfolio Returns per Deviation and Size Quartiles (GARCH)

This table corresponds to Table A.6, but presents the results for GARCH specification. For a description of the table content, refer to Table 13, Section 5.4.2, in the main text.

Panel A: 3-factor abnormal returns

'1 Year' portfolio time-series (236 months)

	Big		Q2		Q3		Small		Small - Big	
Deviation Quartile	Abnormal Return	t-stat	Abnormal Return	t-stat	Abnormal Return	t-stat	Abnormal Return	t-stat	Abnormal Return	t-stat
Lowest	0.85%	2.50	0.54%	1.53	0.13%	0.33	-1.13%	-2.44	-1.78%	-3.11
Q2	0.50%	1.92	0.62%	2.44	0.02%	0.05	-0.40%	-1.07	-1.94%	-5.57
Q3	-0.25%	-0.96	-0.20%	-0.66	-0.09%	-0.25	-0.62%	-1.39	-0.70%	-1.11
Highest	-0.51%	-1.09	-0.87%	-2.37	-0.68%	-1.88	-1.71%	-2.97	-1.14%	-1.88
High - Low	-1.78%	-3.03	-1.08%	-2.34	-0.98%	-1.92	-0.36%	-0.50		

'2 Year' portfolio time-series (270 months)

	Big		Q2		Q3		Small		Small - Big	
Deviation Quartile	Abnormal Return	t-stat	Abnormal Return	t-stat	Abnormal Return	t-stat	Abnormal Return	t-stat	Abnormal Return	t-stat
Lowest	0.76%	2.96	0.11%	0.48	-0.29%	-1.11	-0.79%	-1.73	-1.44%	-2.69
Q2	0.37%	2.03	0.02%	0.09	-0.69%	-2.97	-1.06%	-2.51	-1.42%	-3.08
Q3	-0.30%	-1.56	-0.64%	-2.74	-0.73%	-2.35	-1.44%	-3.89	-0.58%	-1.16
Highest	-0.50%	-1.69	-0.73%	-2.80	-1.18%	-4.49	-1.27%	-2.58	-0.38%	-0.79
High - Low	-1.29%	-3.54	-0.62%	-2.15	-0.78%	-2.16	-0.06%	-0.12		

'3 Year' portfolio time-series (274 months)

	Big		Q2		Q3		Small		Small - Big	
Deviation Quartile	Abnormal Return	t-stat	Abnormal Return	t-stat	Abnormal Return	t-stat	Abnormal Return	t-stat	Abnormal Return	t-stat
Lowest	0.55%	2.52	0.12%	0.59	-0.37%	-1.33	0.01%	0.01	-0.84%	-1.31
Q2	0.29%	1.68	-0.18%	-0.87	-0.66%	-2.97	-0.46%	-0.89	-0.69%	-1.28
Q3	-0.15%	-0.82	-0.39%	-1.94	-0.52%	-1.79	-0.50%	-1.18	-0.33%	-0.76
Highest	-0.36%	-1.46	-0.72%	-3.04	-1.03%	-3.69	-0.16%	-0.27	-0.35%	-0.78
High - Low	-1.02%	-3.00	-0.79%	-2.84	-0.57%	-1.91	-0.97%	-2.09		

Panel B: 4-factor abnormal returns

'1 Year' portfolio time-series (236 months)

	Big		Q2		Q3		Small		Small - Big	
Deviation Quartile	Abnormal Return	t-stat	Abnormal Return	t-stat	Abnormal Return	t-stat	Abnormal Return	t-stat	Abnormal Return	t-stat
Lowest	0.73%	2.11	0.65%	1.70	0.21%	0.56	-1.13%	-2.43	-1.76%	-3.20
Q2	0.48%	1.89	0.58%	2.24	0.01%	0.03	-0.67%	-1.88	-2.08%	-5.62
Q3	-0.24%	-0.91	-0.23%	-0.80	-0.17%	-0.50	-1.07%	-2.22	-0.84%	-1.29
Highest	-0.51%	-1.21	-1.08%	-2.95	-0.77%	-2.18	-2.35%	-4.98	-1.54%	-2.45
High - Low	-1.70%	-3.41	-1.38%	-2.95	-1.13%	-2.23	-1.34%	-1.94		

'2 Year' portfolio time-series (270 months)

	Big		Q2		Q3		Small		Small - Big	
Deviation Quartile	Abnormal Return	t-stat	Abnormal Return	t-stat	Abnormal Return	t-stat	Abnormal Return	t-stat	Abnormal Return	t-stat
Lowest	0.83%	3.36	0.12%	0.51	-0.33%	-1.24	-1.11%	-2.12	-2.11%	-4.53
Q2	0.40%	2.10	-0.03%	-0.13	-0.71%	-2.85	-1.18%	-3.22	-1.65%	-4.31
Q3	-0.31%	-1.57	-0.84%	-2.89	-0.61%	-2.42	-0.96%	-1.96	-0.74%	-1.52
Highest	-0.58%	-2.10	-0.83%	-3.55	-1.14%	-4.18	-1.48%	-3.86	-0.77%	-1.56
High - Low	-1.31%	-3.72	-0.82%	-2.78	-0.96%	-2.79	-0.43%	-0.86		

'3 Year' portfolio time-series (274 months)

	Big		Q2		Q3		Small		Small - Big	
Deviation Quartile	Abnormal Return	t-stat	Abnormal Return	t-stat	Abnormal Return	t-stat	Abnormal Return	t-stat	Abnormal Return	t-stat
Lowest	0.57%	2.68	0.12%	0.62	-0.44%	-1.61	-0.22%	-0.36	-1.02%	-1.95
Q2	0.33%	1.88	-0.23%	-1.12	-0.72%	-3.41	-0.89%	-2.56	-1.37%	-3.83
Q3	-0.15%	-0.82	-0.46%	-2.28	-0.87%	-3.15	-0.62%	-1.10	-0.80%	-1.83
Highest	-0.49%	-1.97	-0.96%	-4.32	-1.12%	-5.10	-0.83%	-1.29	0.03%	0.04
High - Low	-1.04%	-3.27	-0.99%	-3.21	-0.76%	-2.79	-1.08%	-2.20		

Bibliography

Aboody, D., J. Hughes, and J. Liu (2005). Earnings quality, insider trading, and cost of capital. *Journal of Accounting Research 43*, 651–673.

Alford, A. (1992). The effect of the set of comparable firms on the accuracy of the price-earnings valuation method. *Journal of Accounting Research 30*, 94–108.

Altman, E. (1968). Financial ratios, discriminant analysis and the prediction of corporate bankruptcy. *Journal of Finance 23*, 589–609.

Banz, R. (1981). The relationship between return and market value of common stocks. *Journal of Financial Economics 9*, 3–18.

Barber, B. and J. Lyon (1997). Detecting long-run abnormal stock returns: The empirical power and specification of test statistics. *Journal of Financial Economics 43*, 341–372.

Beneish, M. (1997). Detecting gaap violation: Implications for assessing earnings management among firms with extreme financial performance. *Journal of Accounting and Public Policy 16*, 271–309.

Benninga, S., M. Helmantel, and O. Sarig (2005). The timing of initial public offerings. *Journal of Financial Economics 75*, 115–132.

Bernard, V. (1987). Cross-sectional dependence and problems in inference in market-based accounting research. *Journal of Accounting Research 25*, 1–48.

Botosan, C. (1997). Disclosure level and the cost of equity capital. *The Accounting Review 72*, 323–349.

Brav, A. (2000). Inference in long-horizon event studies: A bayesian approach with application to initial public offerings. *Journal of Finance 55*, 1979–2016.

Brav, A., C. Geczy, and P. Gompers (2000). Is the abnormal return following equity issuances anomalous? *Journal of Financial Economics 56*, 209–249.

Brav, A. and P. Gompers (1997). Myth or reality? the long-run underperformance of initial public offerings: evidence from venture and nonventure capital-backed companies. *Journal of Finance 52*, 1791–1821.

Breeden, D. (1979). An intertemporal asset pricing model with stochastic consumption and investment opportunities. *Journal of Financial Economics 7*, 265–296.

Brock, W., J. Lakonishok, and B. LeBaron (1992). Simple technical trading rules and the stochastic properties of stock returns. *Journal of Finance 47*, 1731–1764.

Carhart, M. (1997). On the persistence of mutual fund performance. *Journal of Finance 52*, 57–82.

Chan, L., N. Jegadeesh, and J. Lakonishok (1995). Evaluating the performance of value versus glamour stocks - the impact of selection bias. *Journal of Financial Economics 38*, 269–296.

Chemmanur, T. and I. Paeglis (2005). Management quality, certification, and initial public offerings. *Journal of Financial Economics 76*, 331–368.

Conrad, J. and G. Kaul (1993). Long-term market overreaction or biases in computed returns? *Journal of Finance 48*, 39–63.

DeBondt, W. and R. Thaler (1985). Does the stock market overreact? *Journal of Finance 40*, 793–805.

Dechow, P. and I. Dichev (2002). The quality of accruals and earnings: The role of accrual estimation errors. *The Accounting Review 77 Supplement*, 35–59.

DeGroot, M. (1970). *Optimal statistical decisions.* McGraw-Hill, New York.

DuCharme, L., P. Malatesta, and S. Sefcik (2004). Earnings management, stock issues, and shareholder lawsuits. *Journal of Financial Economics 71*, 27–49.

Easley, D., S. Hvidkjær, and M. O'Hara (2002). Is information risk a determinant of assets returns? *Journal of Finance 57*, 2185–2221.

Easley, D., N. Kiefer, and M. O'Hara (1996). Cream-skimming or profit-sharing? The curious role of purchased order flow. *Journal of Finance 51*, 811–833.

Easley, D. and M. O'Hara (2004). Information and the cost of capital. *Journal of Finance 59*, 1553–1583.

Eckbo, B., R. Masulis, and Ø. Norli (2000). Seasoned public offerings: resolution of the 'new issues puzzle'. *Journal of Financial Economics 56*, 251–291.

Eckbo, B. and Ø. Norli (2005). Liquidity risk, leverage and long-run IPO returns. *Journal of Corporate Finance 11*, 1–35.

Ecker, F., J. Francis, I. Kim, P. Olsson, and K. Schipper (2006). A returns-based representation of earnings quality. *The Accounting Review 81*, 749–780.

Ecker, F., J. Francis, P. Olsson, and K. Schipper (2005). Comparing total and current accruals quality. Duke University working paper.

Fama, E. (1970). Efficient capital markets: A review of theory and empirical work. *Journal of Finance 25*, 383–417.

Fama, E. (1976). *Foundations of Finance.* Basic Books Inc. New York.

Fama, E. (1996). Multifactor portfolio efficiency and multifactor asset pricing. *Journal of Financial and Quantitative Analysis 31*, 441–465.

Fama, E. (1998). Market efficiency, long-term returns, and behavioral finance. *Journal of Financial Economics 49*, 283–306.

Fama, E. and K. French (1992). The cross-section of expected stock returns. *Journal of Finance 47*, 427–465.

Fama, E. and K. French (1993). Common risk factors in the returns on stocks and bonds. *Journal of Financial Economics 33*, 3–56.

Fama, E. and K. French (1995). Size and book-to-market in earnings and returns. *Journal of Finance 50*, 131–155.

Fama, E. and K. French (1996a). Multifactor explanations of asset pricing anomalies. *Journal of Finance 51*, 55–84.

Fama, E. and K. French (1996b). The CAPM is wanted, dead or alive. *Journal of Finance 51*, 1947–1958.

Fama, E. and K. French (1997). Industry costs of equity. *Journal of Financial Economics 43*, 153–193.

Francis, J., R. LaFond, P. Olsson, and K. Schipper (2004a). Costs of equity and earnings attributes. *The Accounting Review 79*, 967–1010.

Francis, J., R. LaFond, P. Olsson, and K. Schipper (2004b). Financial anomalies and information uncertainty. Duke University working paper.

Francis, J., R. LaFond, P. Olsson, and K. Schipper (2005). The market pricing of accruals quality. *Journal of Accounting and Economics 39*, 295–327.

Francis, J., K. Schipper, and L. Vincent (2003). The relative and incremental explanatory power of earnings and alternative (to earnings) performance measures for returns. *Contemporary Accounting Research 20*, 121–164.

Guay, W., S. Kothari, and R. Watts (1996). A market-based evaluation of discretionary accrual models. *Journal of Accounting Research 34 (Supplement)*, 83–105.

Gujarati, D. (2003). *Basic Econometrics* (4th edition ed.). McGraw-Hill Inc., New York.

Haugen, R. (1995). *The New Finance: The Case against Efficient Markets.* Prentice Hall, Englewood Cliffs, NJ.

Hou, K., P. Olsson, and D. Robinson (2001). Does takeover increase stockholder value? Duke University working paper.

Ikenberry, D., J. Lakonishok, and T. Vermaelen (1995). Market underreaction to open market share repurchases. *Journal of Financial Economics 39*, 181–208.

Jaffe, J. (1974). Special information and insider trading. *Journal of Business 47*, 410–428.

Jegadeesh, N. and S. Titman (1993). Returns to buying winners and selling losers: Implications for stock market efficiency. *Journal of Finance 48*, 65–91.

Jensen, M. (1969). Risk, the pricing of capital assets, and the evaluation of investment portfolios. *Journal of Business 42*, 167–247.

Jones, J. (1991). Earnings management during import relief investigations. *Journal of Accounting Research 29*, 193–228.

Kim, M. and J. Ritter (1999). Valuing IPOs. *Journal of Financial Economics 53*, 409–437.

Kothari, S., J. Shanken, and R. Sloan (1995). Another look at the cross-section of expected stock returns. *Journal of Finance 50*, 185–224.

Kothari, S. and J. Warner (1997). Measuring long-horizon security price performance. *Journal of Financial Economics 43*, 301–339.

Lakonishok, J., A. Shleifer, and R. Vishny (1994). Contrarian investment, extrapolation, and risk. *Journal of Finance 49*, 1541–1578.

Lambert, R., C. Leuz, and R. Verrecchia (2006). Information asymmetry, information precision and the cost of capital. University of Pennsylvania working paper.

Lintner, J. (1965). The valuation of risk assets and the selection of risky investments in stock portfolios and capital budgets. *Review of Economics and Statistics 47*, 13–37.

Liu, J., D. Nissim, and J. Thomas (2002). Equity valuation using multiples. *Journal of Accounting Research 40*, 135–172.

Loughran, T. (1997). Book-to-market across firm size, exchange, and seasonality: Is there an effect? *Journal of Financial and Quantitative Analysis 32*, 249–268.

Loughran, T. and J. Ritter (1995). The new issues puzzle. *Journal of Finance 50*, 23–51.

Loughran, T. and J. Ritter (2000). Uniformly least powerful tests of market efficiency. *Journal of Financial Economics 55*, 361–389.

Loughran, T. and J. Ritter (2004). Why has IPO underpricing changed over time? *Financial Management 33*, 5–37.

Lowry, M. and G. Schwert (2004). Is the IPO pricing process efficient? *Journal of Financial Economics 71*, 3–26.

Lyon, J., B. Barber, and C. Tsai (1999). Improved methods for tests of long-run abnormal stock returns. *Journal of Finance 54*, 165–201.

MacKinlay, C. (1995). Multifactor models do not explain deviations from the CAPM. *Journal of Financial Economics 38*, 3–28.

Mandelker, G. (1974). Risk and return: The case of merging firms. *Journal of Financial Economics 1*, 303–335.

McNichols, M. (2002). Discussion of 'the quality of accruals and earnings: the role of accrual estimation errors.'. *The Accounting Review 77 (Supplement)*, 61–69.

Merton, R. (1973). An intertemporal capital asset pricing model. *Econometrica 41*, 867–887.

Merton, R. (1987). A simple model of capital market equilibrium with incomplete information. *Journal of Finance 42*, 483–510.

Miller, E. (1977). Risk, uncertainty, and divergence of opinion. *Journal of Finance 32*, 1151–1168.

Mitchell, M. and E. Stafford (2000). Managerial decisions and long-term stock price performance. *Journal of Business 73*, 287–329.

Morris, S. (1996). Speculative investor behavior and learning. *Quarterly Journal of Economics 111*, 1111–1133.

O'Hara, M. (2003). Presidential address: Liquidity and price discovery. *Journal of Finance 58*, 1335–1354.

Rao, G. (1993). The relation between stock returns and earnings: A study of newly-public firms. Kidder Peabody and Co. working paper.

Ritter, J. (1991). The long-term performance of initial public offerings. *Journal of Finance 46*, 3–27.

Ritter, J. (1998). Initial public offerings. In WGL (Ed.), *Handbook of modern finance*, pp. 5–30. John Wiley & Sons., New York.

Ritter, J. (2002). Investment banking and securities issuance. In G. Constantinides, M. Harris, and R. Stulz (Eds.), *Handbook of the economics of finance*, pp. 253–304. John Wiley & Sons., New York.

Ritter, J. and I. Welch (2002). A review of ipo activity, pricing, and allocations. *Journal of Finance 57*, 1795–1828.

Ross, S. (1976). The arbitrage theory of capital asset pricing. *Journal of Economic Theory 13*, 341–360.

Schultz, P. (2001). The timing of initial public offerings. University of Notre Dame working paper.

Schultz, P. (2003). Pseudo market timing and the long-run underperformance of IPOs. *Journal of Finance 58*, 483–517.

Sharpe, W. (1964). Capital asset prices: A theory of market equilibrium under conditions of risk. *Journal of Finance 19*, 425–442.

Spiess, D. and J. Affleck-Graves (1995). Underperformance in long-run stock returns following seasoned equity offerings. *Journal of Financial Economics 38*, 243–267.

Stattman, D. (1980). Book values and stock returns. *The Chicago MBA: A Journal of Selected Papers 4*, 25–45.

Teoh, S., I. Welch, and T. Wong (1998). Earnings management and the long-run market performance of initial public offerings. *Journal of Finance 53*, 1935–1974.

Teoh, S., T. Wong, and G. Rao (1998). Are accruals during initial public offerings opportunistic? *Review of Accounting Studies 3*, 175–208.

Tsay, R. (2002). *Analysis of financial time series.* John Wiley Sons. New York.

GPSR Compliance

The European Union's (EU) General Product Safety Regulation (GPSR) is a set of rules that requires consumer products to be safe and our obligations to ensure this.

If you have any concerns about our products, you can contact us on ProductSafety@springernature.com

In case Publisher is established outside the EU, the EU authorized representative is:

Springer Nature Customer Service Center GmbH
Europaplatz 3
69115 Heidelberg, Germany

FSC
www.fsc.org
MIX
Papier | Fördert gute Waldnutzung
FSC® C083411

Kolibri 360 GmbH
Ferdinand-Jühlke-Straße 7
99095 Erfurt, Deutschland
produktsicherheit@kolibri360.de